The eXplainable A.I.:

With Python Examples

Disclaimer

The opinions expressed in this book are those of the author. They do not purport to reflect the opinions or views of the companies that the author has worked for or consulted with.

About the Author

Chris Kuo has been a quantitative professional for more than 20 years. During that time, he contributed various data science solutions to industrial operations including customer analytics, risk segmentation, insurance pricing, underwriting, claims, workers compensation, fraud detection, and litigation. He is the inventor of a U.S. patent. He has worked at the Hartford Insurance Group (HIG), the American International Group (AIG), Liberty Mutual Insurance, the BJ's Wholesale Club, and Brookstone Inc.

Chris Kuo is a passionate educator. He has been an adjunct professor at Columbia University, Boston University, University of New Hampshire, and Liberty University since 2001. He published articles in economic and management journals and served as a journal reviewer for related journals. He is the author of *The eXplainable A.I.*, *Modern Time Series Anomaly Detection: With Python & R Code Examples*, and *Transfer Learning for Image Classification: With Python Examples*. He is known as Dr. Dataman on Medium.com.

He received his undergraduate degree in Nuclear Engineering from TsingHua National University in Taiwan, and his Ph.D. in Economics from the State University of New York at Stony Brook. He lives in New York City with his wife France. He can be reached at ck2869@columbia.edu.

"Family life, working, teaching, and writing have filled me with great wonders. As I was writing this book, my wife

Frances was busy taking care of all the daily chores. It wouldn't come to realization without her praying hands and unfaltering support.

~ Chris Kuo, New York

Table of Contents

6

Preface

Artificial intelligence (AI) has been integrated into every part of our lives. A chatbot, enabled by advanced Natural language processing (NLP), pops to assist you while you surf a webpage. A voice recognition system can authenticate you in order to unlock your account. A drone or driverless car can service operations or access areas that are humanly impossible. Machine-learning (ML) predictions are utilized in all decision makings. A broad range of industries such as manufacturing, healthcare, finance, law enforcement, and education rely more and more on AI-enabled systems.

How AI systems make the decisions is not known to most people. Many of the algorithms, though achieving high-level of precision, are not easily understandable for how a recommendation is made. This is especially the case in a deep learning model. As humans, we must be able to fully understand how decisions are being made so that we can trust the decisions of AI systems. We need ML models to function as expected, to produce transparent explanations, and to be visible in how they work. **Explainable AI (XAI)** is important research and has been guiding the development of AI. It enables humans to understand the models so as to manage effectively the benefits that AI systems provide, while maintaining a high level of prediction accuracy. Explainable AI answers the following questions to build the trusts of users for the AI systems:

- Why does the model predict that result?

- What are the reasons for a prediction?
- What is the prediction interval?
- How does the model work?

Who this book is for

This book is for data science professionals who want to get your AI systems or complex machine learning models adopted. This book is certainly suitable for students who are coming to this profession.

What this book covers

The book provides both theoretical motivation as well as hands-on code examples.

Chapter 1, Explain Your Model with the SHAP Values, informs you how you can use the SHAP values to explain your machine learning model, and how the SHAP values work. You will be motivated to apply it to your use cases.

Chapter 2, The SHAP with More Elegant Charts, presents more chart ideas for practitioners to deliver to their audiences.

Chapter 3, How Is the Partial Dependent Plot Calculated, gives the step-by-step explanation for a partial dependence plot.

Chapter 4, Explain Any Model with the SHAP Values - Use the KernelExplainer,
informs the readers that there is one single algorithm for different machine learning models.

Chapter 5, The SHAP Values with H2O Models, shows how the H2O module, a popular package, produces the SHAP values.

Chapter 6, Explain Your Model with Microsoft's interpretML, informs you why the InterpretML uses the Generalized Additive Model (GAM) as the tool to build an explainable model.

Chapter 7, Explain Your Model with LIME, equips you with the LIME method. You will appreciate the challenges the LIME argues and its approach.

How to use this book

I have attempted to make the chapters more independent of each other. But there is a minimum core that is necessary before exploring other chapters.

- ☒ **Minimum core:** Readers who want to survey different methods (SHAP, LIME, and InterpretML) can cover Chapter 1, 6, 7.
- ☒ **The SHAP series:** Readers who want to focus on the SHAP values are recommended to cover Chapter 1, 2, 4, 5.
- ☒ **Theoretical motivation:** Readers who want to learn the theoretical motivation are recommended to cover Chapter 1, 3, 5, 7.

Download the example code

Although the code is in the code box, we do not expect you key in the code. The Python file is available in the GitHub folder:

https://github.com/dataman-git/The-explainable-ai
Readers can key in the above address in the address bar of a
browser to access all the code examples.

Conventions used

There are a few text conventions throughout this book.

- ☒ `Code`: Code words, database table names, file names, or
  URLs are presented with the `Courier New Font`.
- ☒ **Bold:** Any important words or terms are bolded.
- ☒ For easy access, this book uses hyperlinks in each chapter.

Datasets in this book

The red wine quality data in Kaggle.com will be used throughout
this book. This lets readers focus on algorithms and spend less
time in familiarizing new data. Readers can also compare the
modeling outcomes in different chapters.

Errata

Although this book has taken the necessary care to ensure the
accuracy of the content, mistakes or software updates do
happen. If you have found a mistake in the book, please kindly
share with me.

Chapter 1: Explain Your Model with the SHAP Values

"Creativity is thinking up new things. Innovation is doing new things." ~ Professor Theodore Levitt, Harvard Business School

All the machine models need to be explainable. Is your highly trained model easy to understand? A sophisticated machine learning algorithm usually can produce accurate predictions, but its notorious "black box" nature does not help adoption at all. Think about this: If you ask me to swallow a black pill without telling me what's in it, I certainly don't want to swallow it. The interpretability of a model is like a label on a drug bottle. We need to make our effective pill transparent for easy adoption.

The *SHAP value* is a great tool to explain the prediction by your machine learning model. The SHAP value emerges from the Shapley value. In this chapter I will first explain what the Shapley value is, and how the SHAP (SHapley Additive exPlanations) value emerges from the Shapley concept. After that, I will build a random forest model, then apply the SHAP values to explain the predictions of the random forest model.

(A) What is the Shapley Value?

Let me describe the Shapley value with a story: Assume Ann, Bob, and Cindy together were hammering an "error" wood log, 38 inches, to the ground. After work, they went to a local bar for a drink and I, a mathematician, came to join them. I asked a very bizarre question: "What is everyone's contribution (in inches)?"

How to answer this question? I listed all the permutations and came up with the data in Table (A). (Some of you already asked me how to come up with this table. See my note at the end of the chapter.) When the ordering is A, B, C, the marginal contributions of the three are 2, 32, and 4 inches respectively.

Combination	Marginal contribution			inches
	Ann	Bob	Cindy	Total
A, B, C	2	32	4	38
A, C, B	4	34	0	38
B, A, C	2	32	4	38
B, C, A	0	28	10	38
C, A, B	2	36	0	38
C, B, A	0	28	10	38
Average	2	32	4	38

Table (A)

Table (A) shows the coalition of (A,B) or (B,A) is 34 inches, so the marginal contribution of C to this coalition is 4 inches. I took the average of all the permutations for each person to get each individual's contribution: Ann is 2 inches, Bob is 32 inches and Cindy is 4 inches. That's the way to calculate the Shapley value: It is the average of the marginal contributions across all permutations. I will describe the calculation in the formal mathematical term at the end of this post. But now, let's see how it is applied in machine learning.

I called the wood log the "error" log for a special reason: It is the loss function in the context of machine learning. The "error" is the difference between the actual value and prediction. The hammers are the predictors to attack the error log. How do we measure the contributions of the hammers (predictors)? The Shapley values.

(B) From the Shapley Value to SHAP (SHapley Additive exPlanations)

The SHAP (SHapley Additive exPlanations) deserves its own space rather than an extension of the Shapley value. Inspired by several methods [1],[2],[3],[4],[5],[6] on model interpretability, Lundberg and Lee [7] proposed the SHAP value as a united approach to explaining the output of any machine learning model. Three benefits worth mentioning here.

1. The first one is *global interpretability* — the collective SHAP values can show how much each predictor contributes, either positively or negatively, to the target variable. This is like the variable importance plot, but it is able to show the positive or negative relationship for each variable with the target (see the SHAP value plot below).
2. The second benefit is *local interpretability* — each observation gets its own set of SHAP values (see the individual SHAP value plot below). This greatly increases its transparency. We can explain why a case receives its prediction and the contributions of the predictors. Traditional variable importance algorithms only show the results across the entire population but not on each individual case. The local interpretability enables us to pinpoint and contrast the impacts of the factors.
3. Third, the SHAP values can be calculated for any tree-based model, while other methods use linear regression or logistic regression models as the surrogate models.

(C) How to Use the SHAP in Python?

I will build a random forest regression model and use the `TreeExplainer` in SHAP. I use the <u>red wine quality data</u> in Kaggle.com to build the model. There are 1,599 wine samples. The column for the target is the quality rating from low to high (0–10). The input variables are the content of each wine sample including fixed acidity, volatile acidity, citric acid, residual sugar, chlorides, free sulfur dioxide, total sulfur dioxide, density, pH, sulphates and alcohol.

```
import pandas as pd
import numpy as np
np.random.seed(0)
import matplotlib.pyplot as plt

# Load the data
df = pd.read_csv('/winequality-red.csv')
from sklearn.model_selection import train_test_split
from sklearn import preprocessing
from sklearn.ensemble import RandomForestRegressor

# The target variable is 'quality'.
Y = df['quality']
X = df[['fixed acidity', 'volatile acidity',
        'citric acid', 'residual sugar',
        'chlorides', 'free sulfur dioxide',
        'total sulfur dioxide', 'density',
        'pH', 'sulphates', 'alcohol']]

# Split the data into train and test data:
```

```
X_train, X_test, Y_train, Y_test =
    train_test_split(X, Y, test_size = 0.2)

# Build a random forest model.
model = RandomForestRegressor(max_depth=6,
          random_state=0, n_estimators=10)
model.fit(X_train, Y_train)
```

The above code builds the random forest model as "model". Now we are going to explain the model.

(D) Variable Importance Plot — Global Interpretability

First install the SHAP module by doing `pip install SHAP`. We are going to produce the variable importance plot. A variable importance plot lists the most significant variables in descending order. The top variables contribute more to the model than the bottom ones and thus have high predictive power. The `shap.summary_plot` function with `plot_type="bar"` lets you produce it.

```
import shap
shap_values =
shap.TreeExplainer(model).shap_values(X_train)
shap.summary_plot(shap_values, X_train,
plot_type="bar")
```

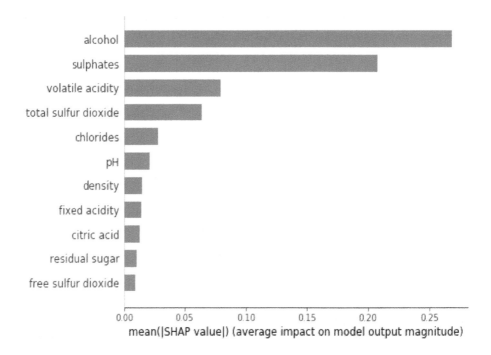

The SHAP value plot can show the positive and negative relationships of the predictors with the target variable. The code `shap.summary_plot(shap_values, X_train)` produces the following plot:

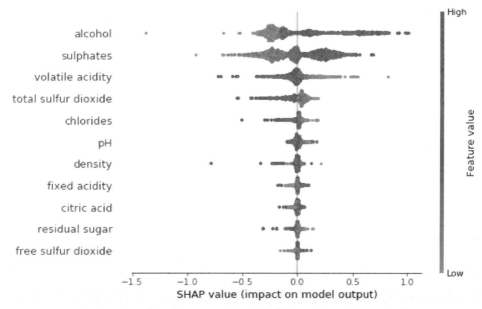

Figure (D.1): The SHAP Variable Importance Plot

This plot is made of all the dots in the train data. It delivers the following information:

- *Feature importance:* Variables are ranked in descending order.
- *Impact:* The horizontal location shows whether the effect of that value *is associated with a higher or lower prediction.*
- *Original value:* Color shows whether that variable is high (in red) or low (in blue) for that observation.
- *Correlation:* A *high* level of the "alcohol" content has a high and positive impact on the quality rating. The "high" comes from the red color, and the "positive" impact is shown on the X-axis. Similarly, we will say the "volatile acidity" is negatively correlated with the target variable.

You may want to save the summary plot. Although the SHAP does not have built-in functions, you can save the plot by using `matplotlib`:

```
import matplotlib.pyplot as plt
f = plt.figure()
shap.summary_plot(rf_shap_values, X_test)
f.savefig("/summary_plot1.png",
          bbox_inches-'tight', dpi=600)
```

(E) SHAP Dependence Plot — Global Interpretability

How to show a **partial dependence plot**? A partial dependence plot shows the marginal effect of one or two features on the predicted outcome of a machine learning model J. H. Friedman [8]. It tells whether the relationship between the target and a feature is linear, monotonic or more complex. I provide more detail in Chapter 3, How Is the Partial Dependent Plot Calculated?

To create a dependence plot, you only need one line of code: `shap.dependence_plot("alcohol", shap_values, X_train)`. The function automatically includes another variable that your chosen variable interacts most with. Figure (E.1) shows there is an approximately linear and positive trend between "alcohol" and the target variable, and "alcohol" interacts with "sulphates" frequently.

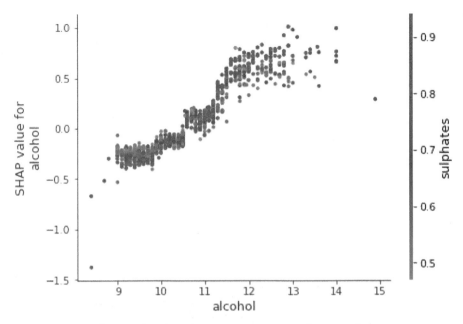

Figure (E.1): The SHAP Dependence Plot

Suppose you want to know "volatile acidity", as well as the variable that it interacts with the most, you can do `shap.dependence_plot("volatile acidity", shap_values, X_train)`. Figure (E.2) shows there exists an approximately linear but negative relationship between "volatile acidity" and the target variable. This negative relationship is also demonstrated in the variable importance plot Figure (D.1).

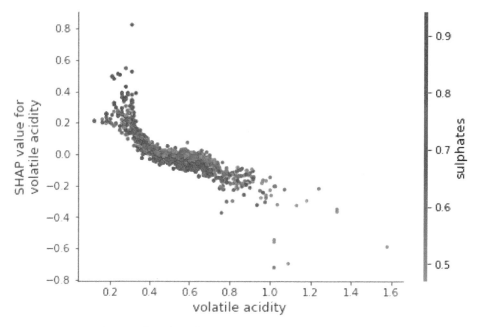

Figure (E.2): The SHAP Dependence Plot

(F) Individual SHAP Value Plot — Local Interpretability

Your machine learning model produces the prediction for a record. How do you make sense of the prediction? The explainability for any individual observation is the most critical step to convince your audience to adopt your model. Let me illustrate the interpretations with several examples. I arbitrarily select some observations and show them in Table (F.1):

```
# Get the predictions and put them with the test
data.
X_output = X_test.copy()
X_output.loc[:,'predict'] =
np.round(model.predict(X_output),2)
```

```
# Randomly pick some observations
random_picks = np.arange(1,330,50) # Every 50 rows
S = X_output.iloc[random_picks]
S
```

	fixed acidity	volatile acidity	citric acid	residual sugar	chlorides	free sulfur dioxide	total sulfur dioxide	density	pH	sulphates	alcohol	predict
1575	7.5	0.520	0.40	2.2	0.060	12.0	20.0	0.99474	3.26	0.64	11.8	6.20
1087	7.9	0.190	0.42	1.6	0.057	18.0	30.0	0.99400	3.29	0.69	11.2	6.18
1031	7.3	0.550	0.01	1.8	0.093	9.0	15.0	0.99514	3.35	0.58	11.0	5.61
724	7.5	1.115	0.10	3.1	0.086	5.0	12.0	0.99580	3.54	0.60	11.2	4.67
59	7.3	0.390	0.31	2.4	0.074	9.0	46.0	0.99620	3.41	0.54	9.4	5.16
147	7.6	0.490	0.26	1.6	0.236	10.0	88.0	0.99680	3.11	0.80	9.3	5.18
893	7.2	0.660	0.03	2.3	0.078	16.0	86.0	0.99743	3.53	0.57	9.7	5.13

Table (F.1): Data S contains some random observations of X_test

You will need to initialize your Jupyter notebook with `initjs()`. To save the repeating work, I write a small function `shap_plot(j)` to produce the SHAP values for several observations in Table (F.1).

```
# Initialize your Jupyter notebook with initjs(),
otherwise you will get an error message.
shap.initjs()

# Write in a function
def shap_plot(j):
    explainerModel    = shap.TreeExplainer(model)
    shap_values_Model =
        explainerModel.shap_values(S)
    p = shap.force_plot(
        explainerModel.expected_value,
```

```
        shap_values_Model[j],
        S.iloc[[j]])
   return(p)
```

(F.1) Interpret Observation 1

Let me walk you through the above code step by step. The `shap.force_plot()` takes three values: (i) the *base value* `explainerModel.expected_value[0]`, (ii) the *SHAP values* `shap_values_Model[j][0]` and (iii) the matrix of feature values `S.iloc[[j]]`. The base value or the expected value is the average of the model output over the training data `X_train`. It is the base value used in the following plot.

When I execute `shap_plot(0)` I get the result for the first row in Table (G.1):

Figure (F.2): Individual SHAP Value Plot for Observation 0 of S

Let me break this elegant plot in detail:

- The *output value* is the prediction for that observation (the prediction of the first row in Table (F.1) is 6.20).

- The *base value*: The original paper [7] explains that the base value E(y_hat) is "the value that would be predicted if we did not know any features for the current output." In other words, it is the mean prediction, or mean(yhat). You may wonder why it is 5.62. This is because the mean prediction of Y_test is 5.62. You can test it out by `Y_test.mean()` which produces 5.62.

- *Red/blue*: Features that push the prediction higher (to the right) are shown in red, and those pushing the prediction lower are in blue.

- Alcohol: has a positive impact on the quality rating. The alcohol content of this wine is 11.8 (as shown in the first row of Table A) which is higher than the average value 10.41. So it pushes the prediction to the right.

- pH: has a negative impact on the quality rating. A lower than the average pH (=3.26 < 3.30) drives the prediction to the right.

- Sulphates: is positively related to the quality rating. A lower than the average Sulphates (= 0.64 < 0.65) pushes the prediction to the left.

- You may wonder how we know the average values of the predictors. Remember the SHAP model is built on the training data set. The means of the variables are: `X_train.mean()`

```
fixed acidity              8.310164
volatile acidity           0.527392
citric acid                0.268444
residual sugar             2.508444
chlorides                  0.087823
free sulfur dioxide       15.885066
total sulfur dioxide      46.455043
density                    0.996726
pH                         3.308702
sulphates                  0.658053
alcohol                   10.416302
dtype: float64
```

Figure (F.3): X_train.mean()

(F.2) Interpret Observation 2

What is the result for the 2nd observation in Table (F.1)? Let's do `shap_plot(1)`:

Figure (F.4): Individual SHAP Value Plot for Observation 1 of S

(F.3) Interpret Observation 3

How about the 3rd observation in Table (F.1)? Let's do `shap_plot(2)`:

Figure (F.5): Individual SHAP Value Plot for Observation 2 of S

26

(F.4) Interpret Observation 4

Just to do one more before you become bored. The 4th observation in Table (F.1) is this: `shap_plot(3)`:

Figure (F.6): Individual SHAP Value Plot for Observation 3 of S

Conclusion

In this chapter we have learned why a model needs to be explainable. We learn the SHAP values, and how the SHAP values help to explain the predictions of your machine learning model. It is helpful to remember the following points:

- ☒ Each feature has a SHAP value contributing to the prediction.
- ☒ The final prediction = the average prediction + the shap values of all features.
- ☒ The shap value of a feature can be positive or negative.
- ☒ If a feature is positively correlated to the target, a value higher than its own average will contribute positively to the prediction.
- ☒ If a feature is negatively correlated to the target, a value higher than its own average will contribute negatively to the prediction.

References

1. Ribeiro, Marco & Singh, Sameer & Guestrin, Carlos. (2016). "Why Should I Trust You?": Explaining the Predictions of Any Classifier. 1135-1144. 10.1145/2939672.2939778.
2. Štrumbelj, E., Kononenko, I. Explaining prediction models and individual predictions with feature contributions. Knowl Inf Syst 41, 647–665 (2014). https://doi.org/10.1007/s10115-013-0679-x
3. Shrikumar, A., Greenside, P. & Kundaje, A.. (2017). Learning Important Features Through Propagating Activation Differences. <i>Proceedings of the 34th International Conference on Machine Learning</i>, in <i>Proceedings of Machine Learning Research</i> 70:3145-3153 Available from https://proceedings.mlr.press/v70/shrikumar17a.html
4. Datta, A., Sen, S., & Zick, Y. (2016). Algorithmic Transparency via Quantitative Input Influence: Theory and Experiments with Learning Systems. 2016 IEEE Symposium on Security and Privacy (SP), 598-617.
5. Bach S, Binder A, Montavon G, Klauschen F, Müller K-R, Samek W (2015) On Pixel-Wise Explanations for Non-Linear Classifier Decisions by Layer-Wise Relevance Propagation. PLoS ONE 10(7): e0130140. https://doi.org/10.1371/journal.pone.0130140
6. Lipovetsky, S., & Conklin, M. (2001). Analysis of regression in game theory approach. Applied Stochastic Models in Business and Industry, 17, 319-330.
7. Lundberg, S. M. & Lee, S.-I. (2017). A Unified Approach to Interpreting Model Predictions. In I. Guyon, U. V.

Luxburg, S. Bengio, H. Wallach, R. Fergus, S. Vishwanathan & R. Garnett (ed.),Advances in Neural Information Processing Systems 30 (pp. 4765--4774) . Curran Associates, Inc. .

8. Friedman, J. H. (2000). Greedy Function Approximation: A Gradient Boosting Machine. Annals of Statistics, 29, 1189--1232.

Chapter 2: The SHAP with More Elegant Charts

"Without craftsmanship, inspiration is a mere reed in the wind." ~ Johannes Brahms, German composer, pianist, and conductor.

A professional realtor once inspired me with his way of house showing. He first showed me the outlook of the house, the quiet neighborhood, the green lawn, and explained the accessibility of the stores. Then he led me to the house to see each room. In the master bedroom, he encouraged me to open the drawers and closets to be amazed by the recessed lights. I started to imagine how I could host a group of guests around the fireplace, the pool table, and kids roasting marshmallows at the backyard firepit.

We present our machine learning models in a similar way. We explain to the users that the entire model makes sense. The relationships of the predictors with the target variable are consistent with the business domain knowledge. This is called the **global interpretability**. Next, we explain that the individual predictions by the model also make sense. We can explain why each case gets the prediction according to the values of predictors. This is called the **local interpretability**. The SHAP values can show both.

Craftsmanship makes things perfect. You may have spent hours polishing slides or graphs to deliver a stylized presentation. In order to let your audience better understand your predictions and then adopt your model, such craftsmanship is certainly worth it. In this chapter we will expand our knowledge for more charts. They are arranged from simple to complex. On global interpretability, we will learn (a) the bar plot, (b) the cohort plot, and (c) the heatmap plot. On local interpretability, we will learn (d) the waterfall plot, (e) the bar plot, (f) the force plot, and (g) the decision plot. Further, I will show you how to use the matplotlib module to customize a SHAP plot. Finally, if you are building a multi-class model in which the target variable has multiple levels, you can use the SHAP values to explain a multi-class model.

(A) Build a XGBoost Model

Let's continue to use the red wine quality dataset. There are 1,599 wine samples, which are divided into 1,279 training samples and 320 test samples. The target value of this dataset is the quality rating from low to high (0–10). The input variables are the content of each wine sample including fixed acidity, volatile acidity, citric acid, residual sugar, chlorides, free sulfur dioxide, total sulfur dioxide, density, pH, sulphates and alcohol.

Let's build a XGBoost model `xgb_model` using the following code.

```
import pandas as pd
import numpy as np
import matplotlib.pyplot as plt
from sklearn.model_selection import train_test_split
import xgboost as xgb
```

```
df = pd.read_csv('/winequality-red.csv')

features = ['fixed acidity', 'volatile acidity',
            'citric acid', 'residual sugar',
            'chlorides', 'free sulfur dioxide',
            'total sulfur dioxide', 'density',
            'pH', 'sulphates', 'alcohol']
Y = df['quality']
X =  df[features]
X_train, X_test, Y_train, Y_test =
train_test_split(X, Y,
        test_size = 0.2, random_state = 1234)
xgb_model = xgb.XGBRegressor(random_state=42)
xgb_model.fit(X_train, Y_train)

# The SHAP Values
import shap
explainer = shap.Explainer(xgb_model)
shap_values = explainer(X_test)
```

(B) Global Interpretability

Below is the summary plot for the XGB model. We have learned in Chapter 1. Just to recap, a summary plot consists of all observations. It shows the variable importance in descending order. The colors show whether that variable is high (in red) or low (in blue) for that observation. The plot below shows the "alcohol" content has a high and positive impact on the quality rating. The "high" comes from the red color, and the "positive" impact is shown on the X-axis. Following this logic, we will say the "volatile acidity" is negatively correlated with the target variable.

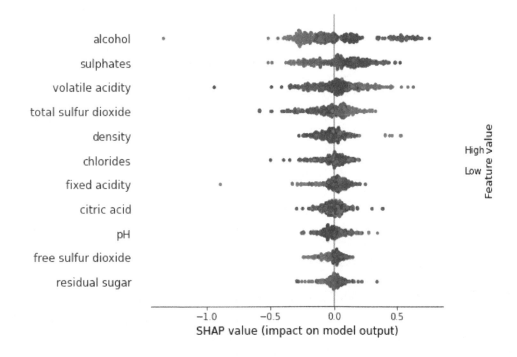

(B.1) Bar plot for feature importance

```
shap.plots.bar(shap_values, max_display=10)
# default is max_display=12
```

If you have too many predictors, the bar plot for the variable importance becomes long and ugly. It does not resonate with your audience and loses its persuasive power. Should you cut off the tail of the chart? But the audience will not know the collective contributions of those less important variables — what if their collective importance is larger than the top variables? The SHAP bar plot lets you specify how many predictors to display and sum up the contributions of the less important variables. This is a nice touch because you can inform the audience of the collective contributions of the rest variables.

33

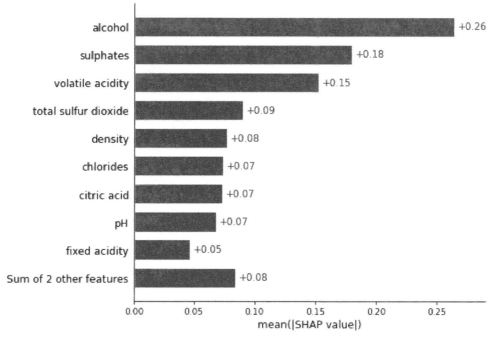

Figure (B.1): The Bar Plot

(B.2) Cohort plot

A population can be divided into two or more groups according to a variable. This gives more insights into the heterogeneity of the population. Figure (B.2) shows my population can be divided into two cohorts: those samples that the alcohol levels are less than 11.15, and those that the alcohol levels are more than 11.15. From Figure (B.1) we know the variable "alcohol" is the most important. Figure (B.2) tells us that the variable "alcohol" is even more important in the second cohort.

This is done by using .cohorts(N) to divide the population into N cohorts. It actually runs sklearn DecisionTreeRegressor for the partition. My population has 320 samples. It is automatically partitioned into 237 samples for one cohort and 83 samples for the second cohort.

```
shap.plots.bar(shap_values.cohorts(2).abs.mean(0))
```

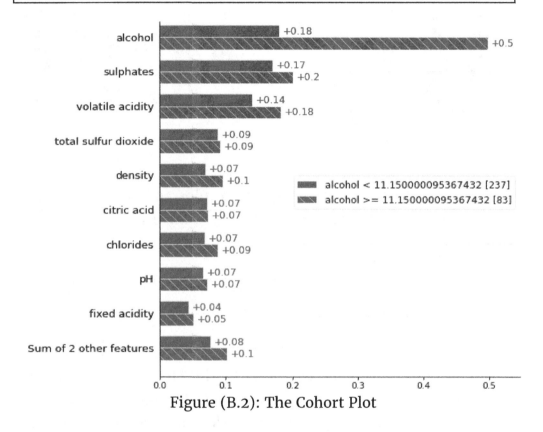

Figure (B.2): The Cohort Plot

The threshold of this optimal division is that alcohol = 11.15. The bar plot tells us that the reason that a wine sample belongs to the cohort of alcohol≥11.15 is because of high alcohol content (SHAP = 0.5), high sulphates (SHAP = 0.2), and high volatile acidity (SHAP = 0.18), etc. This may inspire a market segmentation strategy that the first cohort can be labeled as the "best" selection of wines, and the second cohort as the "value" wine selection.

(B.3) Heatmap plot

Let me arbitrarily choose 100 wine samples and run the following code to create a heatmap. The outcome is in Figure (B.3).

```
shap.plots.heatmap(shap_values[1:100])
```

This heatmap contains much information. First, the importance of the variables is labeled on the left side. The horizontal bars on the right side rank the variables from the most important to the least important. The model variable importance represents the global interpretability. It means this XGBoost model considers "alcohol" as the most important attribute to the wine quality, followed by "sulphates" and so on.

Second, this heatmap is based on wine samples from 1 to 100. So the X-axis is the instance from 1 to 100. The colors show the magnitude of the SHAP values. Look at Wine sample 100 in the right of the heatmap, it has a red color for alcohol, which means "alcohol" has contributed the most to the quality of that wine sample.

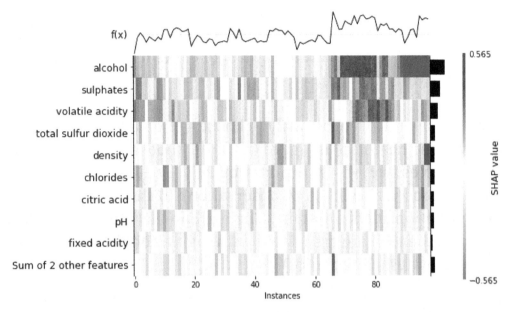

Figure (B.3): The Heatmap for Observation 1 to 100

Third, the *f(x)* curve on the top of Figure (B.3) is the model predictions of the instances. Wine sample 100 has a high prediction. It means the quality of the wine sample 100 is high, and "alcohol" contributes greatly to the quality of that wine sample.

Fourth, you may have noticed the observations have been arranged such that the colors clustered together. This is because the SHAP heatmap class runs a hierarchical clustering on the instances, then orders these 1 to 100 wine samples on the X-axis (using `shap.order.hclust`).

Fifth, the center of the 2D heatmap is the base_value (using `.base_value`), which is the mean prediction for all instances. The heatmap shows high predictions (high values in $f(x)$ to the right) are associated with high alcohol content and high sulphates (in red color).

I mentioned that I "arbitrarily" choose 100 data samples to produce the heatmap in Figure (B.3). If I choose another set of data samples, will the interpretation be very different? In Figure (B.4) I choose another set of observations to show you that the interpretation stays the same. The high predictions (high values in $f(x)$ in the left) are associated with high alcohol content and high sulphates (in red color).

```
shap.plots.heatmap(shap_values[200:300])
```

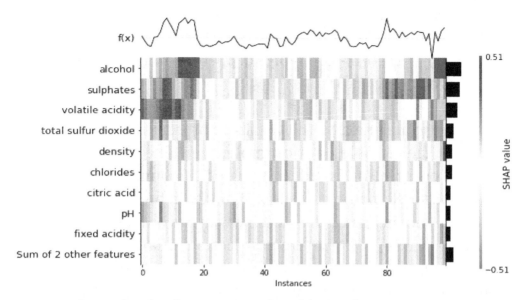

Figure (B.4): The Heatmap for Observation 200 to 300

(C) Local Interpretability

There are many ways to explain an individual prediction. In this section I will demonstrate four types of plots: the waterfall plot, the bar plot, the force plot, and the decision plot. I will repeatedly use two examples (Observation 1 and 2) for each type of plot. This lets you compare how they look.

(C.1) The waterfall plot for Observation 1

A waterfall plot powerfully shows why a case receives its prediction given its variable values. You start with the bottom of a waterfall plot and add (red) or subtract (blue) the values to get to the final prediction. The graph below shows the prediction for the first observation in x_test. It starts with the base value 5.637 in the bottom, which is the average of all observations.

The model prediction for Observation 1 is 4.139, as shown on the top. Why is it 4.139? It is because 5.637−0.04−0.04−0.09+0.09+0.11−0.13−0.27−0.3−0.34−0.5 = 4.139 (notice there is a small rounding error).

There are values next to the variable names. Those are the values of the variables. For example, the value of "alcohol" for the first observation is 9.4. Is 9.4 good, if compared with all other wines? Remember the SHAP model is built on the training data set. The means of the variables can be obtained by X_train.mean(). The average "alcohol" of all wines is 10.41. Observation 1 is only 9.4. Because a high "alcohol" level contributes positively to the quality rating, but the alcohol of Observation 1 is lower than the average, the "alcohol" rating of this wine contributes negatively to its quality prediction by -0.3 as shown in Figure (C.1).

```
fixed acidity          8.310164
volatile acidity       0.527392
citric acid            0.268444
residual sugar         2.508444
chlorides              0.087823
free sulfur dioxide   15.885066
total sulfur dioxide  46.455043
density                0.996726
pH                     3.308702
sulphates              0.658053
alcohol               10.416302
dtype: float64
```

```
# For the first observation
shap.plots.waterfall(shap_values[0])
```

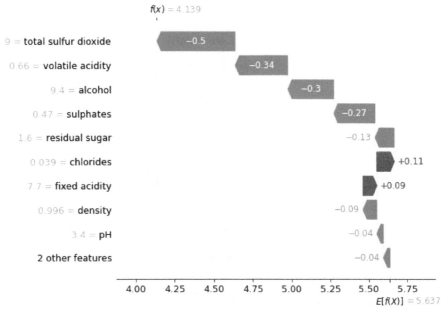

Figure (C.1): The Waterfall Plot for Observation 1

(C.2) The waterfall plot for Observation 2

Below I show the prediction for the second observation in
X_test. The reason that the final prediction is 5.582 is because
5.637+0.01+0.03−0.03+0.04+0.1+0.12−0.12−0.15+0.24−0.29 =
5.582.

```
# For the second observation
shap.plots.waterfall(shap_values[1])
```

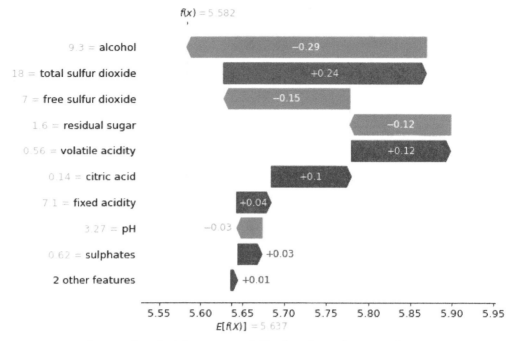

Figure (C.2): The Waterfall Plot for Observation 2

(C.3) The bar plot for Observation 1

Compared with the waterfall plot, the bar plot centers at zero to show the contributions of variables. See Figure (C.3).

```
# For the first observation
shap.plots.bar(shap_values[0])
```

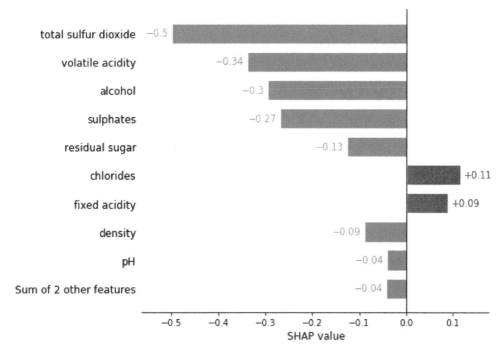

Figure (C.3): The Bar Plot for Observation 1

(C.4) The bar plot for Observation 2

```
# For the second observation
shap.plots.bar(shap_values[1])
```

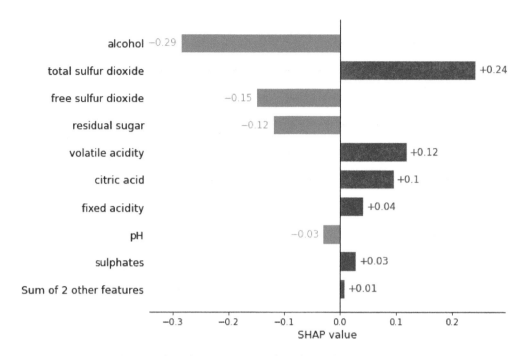

Figure (C.4): The Bar Plot for Observation 2

(C.5) The force plot for Observation 1

We have seen the force plots in <u>Chapter 1 Explain Your Model with the SHAP Values</u>. So here I do not repeat the description. For Observation 1, our XGBoost model predicts it to be 4.14. Why does the model predict it to be 4.14? The force plot in Figure (C.5) starts with the base value 5.637. Those blue factors push the prediction to the left, and the red factors push the prediction to the right. Thus, it settles at 4.14.

```
explainer = shap.TreeExplainer(xgb_model)
shap_values = explainer.shap_values(X_test)
shap.initjs()
def p(j):
```

```
      return(shap.force_plot(explainer.expected_value,
shap_values[j,:], X_test.iloc[j,:]))
p(0)
```

Figure (C.5): The Force Plot for Observation 1

(C.6) The force plot for Observation 2

The prediction for Observation 2 is 5.58. The force plot in Figure (C.6) explains the key factors.

```
p(1)
```

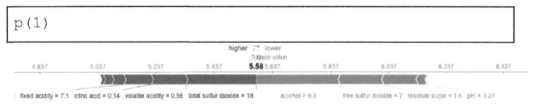

Figure (C.6): The Force Plot for Observation 2

(C.7) The decision plot for Observation 1

If there are many predictors, the force plot becomes busy and does not present them well. A decision plot will be a good choice. Figure (C.7) shows the decision plot for Observation 1. It states that the final prediction is 4.139 (~4.14). The vertical line in the center is the base value. The numbers in parenthesis are the values of the variables. For example, the value of "alcohol" for Observation 1 is 9.4. We know the level of alcohol content positively contributes to the quality of wine. Is 9.4 good, if compared with all other wines? We have explained in Section

(C.1.1) that the means of the variables can be obtained by
`X_train.mean()`. The average "alcohol" of all wines is 10.41
but Observation 1 is only 9.4. Because the alcohol of Observation
1 is lower than the average, the "alcohol" rating of this wine
contributes negatively to its quality prediction, as shown in
Figure (C.7).

```
expected_value = explainer.expected_value
print("The expected value is ", expected_value)
shap_values = explainer.shap_values(X_test)[0]
shap.decision_plot(expected_value, shap_values,
X_test)
```

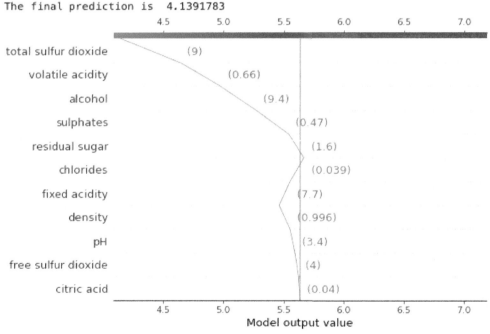

Figure (C.7): The Decision Plot for Observation 1

(C.8) The decision plot for Observation 2

Let's produce the decision plot for Observation 2.

```
shap_values = explainer.shap_values(X_test)[1]
shap.decision_plot(expected_value, shap_values,
X_test)
```

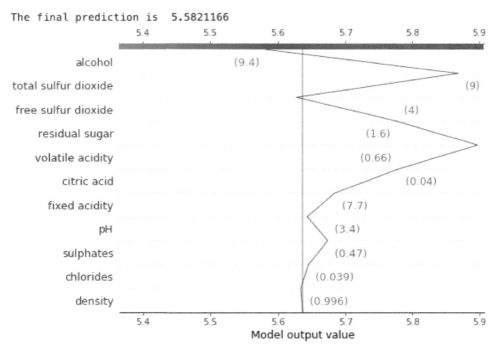

Figure (C.8): The Decision Plot for Observation 2

(D) Binary Target

A binary model can be easily done by specifying `reg:logistic` in `xgb.XGBRegressor()`. The prediction shall be a probability between 0 and 1. However, in the waterfall plot XGBoost presents the log-odds rather than the predicted probability. In this section I want to detail the waterfall plot in the log-odds, and how it can be presented in terms of predicted probability. I will first show you the force plot so you can compare it with the waterfall plot.

(D.1) Force plot

I create a binary target variable `Y = np.where(df['quality']>5,1,0)` and specify `reg:logistic` to build a binary model.

```
from sklearn.model_selection import
train_test_split
import xgboost as xgb

features = ['fixed acidity', 'volatile acidity',
'citric acid', 'residual sugar', 'chlorides',
            'free sulfur dioxide', 'total sulfur
dioxide', 'density', 'pH', 'sulphates', 'alcohol']
Y = np.where(df['quality']>5,1,0)
X =  df[features]

# Train-test-split
X_train, X_test, Y_train, Y_test =
train_test_split(X, Y, test_size = 0.2,
random_state = 1234)

# Build an XGB
xgb_binary_model =
xgb.XGBRegressor(objective='reg:logistic',random_st
ate=42)
xgb_binary_model.fit(X_train, Y_train)
```

```
# Initialize SHAP
shap.initjs()

# A small function
def p(j):
  explainer =
    shap.TreeExplainer(xgb_binary_model)
  xgb_binary_shap_values =
    explainer.shap_values(X_train)

  return(shap.force_plot(
         explainer.expected_value,
         xgb_binary_shap_values[j,:],
         X_train.iloc[j,:], link='logit')
  )
p(0)
```

Below is the force plot for the first observation.

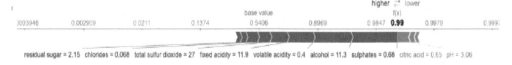

Figure (D.1): The Force Plot of the Binary Model for Observation 1

(D.2) XGBoost with Waterfall plot

```
import shap
explainer = shap.Explainer(xgb_binary_model)
xgb_binary_shap_values = explainer(X_train)
shap.plots.waterfall(xgb_binary_shap_values[0])
```

Below is the waterfall plot. The final prediction in the plot is f(x) = 4.894. We expect the output of this binary model to be a probability between 0 and 1. Why is it larger than 1.0? It is because the units on the x-axis in the waterfall plot are log-odds units rather than probability. The XGBoost classifier produces the margin output before the logistic link function (as explained in its documentation).

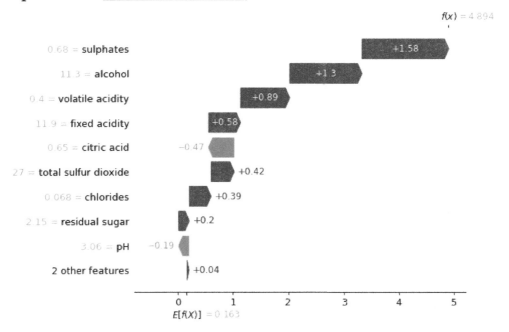

Figure (D.2): The Waterfall Plot of the Binary Model for Observation 1

You can convert the log-odd to a probability of [0,1] by using the logistic sigmoid function, which is expit(x) = 1/(1+exp(-x)), the inverse of the logit function. In other words, 1(1+exp(-4.894)) = 0.992, which is the predicted probability in the force plot in Figure (D.1).

```
def xgb_shap_transform_scale(
      original_shap_values,
      Y_pred,
      which):
   from scipy.special import expit

   # Compute the transformed base value,
   # which consists in applying the logit
   # function to the base value
   # Importing the logit function for the
   # base value transformation
   from scipy.special import expit
   untransformed_base_value =
      original_shap_values.base_values[-1]

   # Computing the original_explanation_distance
   # to construct the distance_coefficient later
   original_explanation_distance =
      np.sum(original_shap_values.values,
      axis=1)[which]
   base_value = expit(untransformed_base_value )

   # Computing the distance between the
   # model_prediction and the transformed
   # base_value
   distance_to_explain = Y_pred[which] - base_value

   # The distance_coefficient is the ratio between
   # both distances which will be used later
   distance_coefficient =
       original_explanation_distance /
       distance_to_explain
```

```
# Transforming the original shapley values to
# the new scale
shap_values_transformed =
original_shap_values / distance_coefficient

# Finally resetting the base_value as it
# does not need to be transformed
shap_values_transformed.base_values =
   base_value
shap_values_transformed.data =
   original_shap_values.data

#Now returning the transformed array
return shap_values_transformed
```

Let's apply the conversion then do the waterfall plot for one observation:

```
obs = 0
Y_pred = xgb_binary_model.predict(X_train)

print("The prediction is ", Y_pred[obs])

shap_values_transformed =
xgb_shap_transform_scale(xgb_binary_shap_values,
Y_pred, obs)
shap.plots.waterfall(shap_values_transformed[obs])
```

Now the waterfall plot is shown as the predicted probabilities.

The prediction is 0.9925615

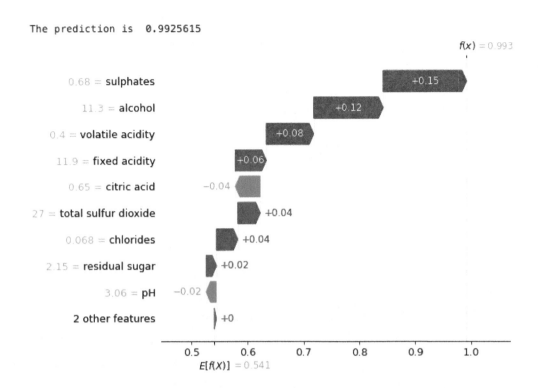

(E) How to Customize SHAP plots

Many SHAP plots can work with Matplotlib for customization. Remember to turn off the plotting parameter of a SHAP function by `show=False`. Below I show an example that the legend masks the graph so we want to move it to a better location. This example divides the population into three cohorts, see Section (B.2) cohort plot for how to do a cohort plot.

(E.1) Legend, fontsize, etc.

```
explainer = shap.Explainer(xgb_model)
shap_values = explainer(X_test)
shap.plots.bar(shap_values.cohorts(3).abs.mean(0))
```

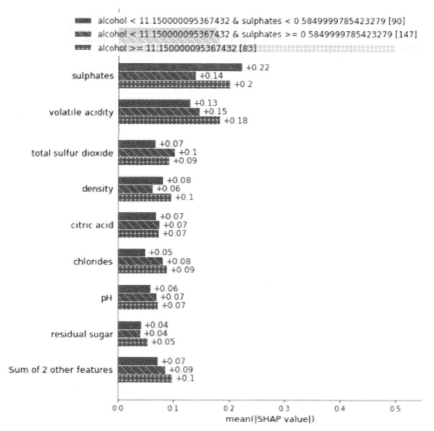

Figure (E.1.1): The legend covers the graph

The location of the legend can be specified by the keyword argument `bbox_to_anchor`, which gives a great degree of control for manual legend placement. See the Legend guide of the Matplotlib.

```
shap.plots.bar(shap_values.cohorts(3).abs.mean(0),
               show=False)
fig = plt.gcf() # gcf means "get current figure"
```

54

```
fig.set_figheight(11)
fig.set_figwidth(9)
#plt.rcParams['font.size'] = '12'
ax = plt.gca() #gca means "get current axes"
leg = ax.legend(bbox_to_anchor=(0., 1.02, 1., .102))
for l in leg.get_texts():
l.set_text(l.get_text().replace('Class', 'Klasse'))
plt.show()
```

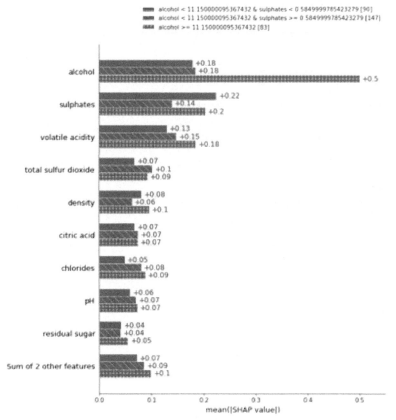

Figure (E.1.2): The legend is above the graph

(E.2) Show SHAP plots in subplots

You may want to present multiple SHAP plots aligning horizontally or vertically. This can be done easily by using the <u>subplot function of Matplotlib</u>.

```python
fig = plt.figure(figsize=(10,5))

ax1 = fig.add_subplot(121)
shap_values = explainer.shap_values(X_test)[0]
shap.decision_plot(expected_value, shap_values,
X_test, show=False)
ax1.title.set_text('The First Observation')

ax2 = fig.add_subplot(122)
shap_values = explainer.shap_values(X_test)[1]
shap.decision_plot(expected_value, shap_values,
X_test, show=False)
ax2.title.set_text('The Second Observation')

plt.tight_layout()
plt.show()
```

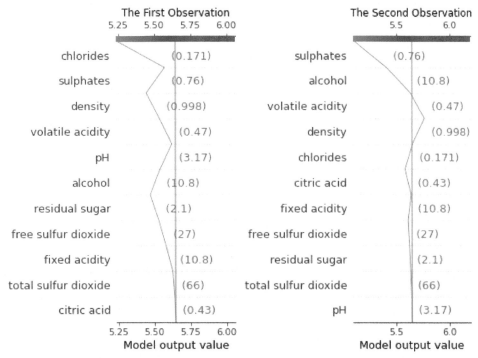

Figure (E.2): Show multiple SHAP plots

(F) The SHAP Plots for a Multi-class Model

You may have built a multi-class model that classifies instances into several classes. How does the SHAP help to demonstrate a multi-class model? Below I create a new target variable 'Multiclass' for three classes: 'Best', 'Premium', and 'Value'. The model is done by specifying `multi:softprob` for the parameter of XGBClassifier.

```
###############################
# Create the Multiclass target  #
# quality > 6: 'Best'            #
```

```
# 5 < quality <= 6: 'Premium'     #
# quality <=5: 'Value'            #
#################################
df['Multiclass'] = np.where(df['quality']>6,
     'Best',
     np.where(df['quality']>5, 'Premium','Value')
     )

Y = df['Multiclass']
X = df[features]

X_train, X_test, Y_train, Y_test =
    train_test_split(X, Y, test_size = 0.2,
    random_state = 1234)

# Build an XGB model
xgb_model =
xgb.XGBClassifier(objective="multi:softprob",
random_state=42)
xgb_model.fit(X_train, Y_train)
```

The output of a multi-class model is a matrix of probabilities for the classes. We have three classes, so the outputs are the probabilities for the three classes, summing up to 1.0. In scikit-learn the function `.predict_proba()` renders the probabilities, as shown in Column "2-Best", "1-Premium" and "0- Value". The function `.predict()` renders the predicted classification, as shown in Column "Pred" below.

```
# Create a dataframe for actual vs. prediction
```

```
multiclass_actual_pred =
    pd.DataFrame(xgb_model.predict_proba(X_test))
    .round(2)
multiclass_actual_pred['Actual'] = Y_test.values
multiclass_actual_pred['Pred'] =
xgb_model.predict(X_test)

multiclass_actual_pred.columns = ['2 - Best','1 -
Premium','0 - Value','Pred','Actual']

# Print out some records
multiclass_actual_pred.head()
```

	2 - Best	1 - Premium	0 - Value	Pred	Actual
0	0.00	0.01	0.99	Value	Value
1	0.00	0.26	0.73	Value	Value
2	0.17	0.76	0.06	Premium	Premium
3	0.00	0.74	0.26	Premium	Premium
4	0.94	0.06	0.00	Best	Best

We can show a confusion matrix like this:

```
pd.crosstab(multiclass_actual_pred['Actual'],
        multiclass_actual_pred['Pred'])
```

Pred Actual	Best	Premium	Value
Best	28	15	1
Premium	10	92	24
Value	3	24	123

You can use the summary plot to show the variable importance by class. Below are two ways to show the results.

```
# Explain the multi-class model using TreeExplainer
import shap
explainer = shap.TreeExplainer(xgb_model)
shap_values =
explainer.shap_values(X_test,approximate=True)

plt.title('The Summary Plot for the Multiclass
Model'+'\n'+'Class 2 - Best, Class 1 - Premium,
Class 0 - Value')

shap.summary_plot(shap_values, X_test,
plot_type="bar")
```

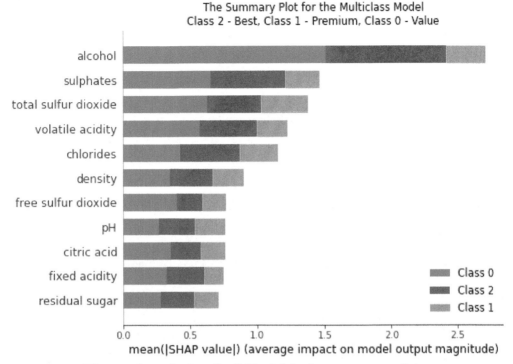

Figure (4.1.1): Stacked Variable importance plots

```
fig = plt.figure(figsize=(20,10))

ax0 = fig.add_subplot(131)
ax0.title.set_text('Class 2 - Best ')
shap.summary_plot(shap_values[2], X_test,
plot_type="bar", show=False)
ax0.set_xlabel(r'SHAP values', fontsize=11)
plt.subplots_adjust(wspace = 5)

ax1 = fig.add_subplot(132)
ax1.title.set_text('Class 1 - Premium')
shap.summary_plot(shap_values[1], X_test,
```

```
plot_type="bar", show=False)
plt.subplots_adjust(wspace = 5)
ax1.set_xlabel(r'SHAP values', fontsize=11)

ax2 = fig.add_subplot(133)
ax2.title.set_text('Class 0 - Value')
shap.summary_plot(shap_values[0], X_test,
plot_type="bar", show=False)
ax2.set_xlabel(r'SHAP values', fontsize=11)

# plt.tight_layout(pad=3) # You can also use
plt.tight_layout() instead of using
plt.subplots_adjust() to add space between plots
plt.show()
```

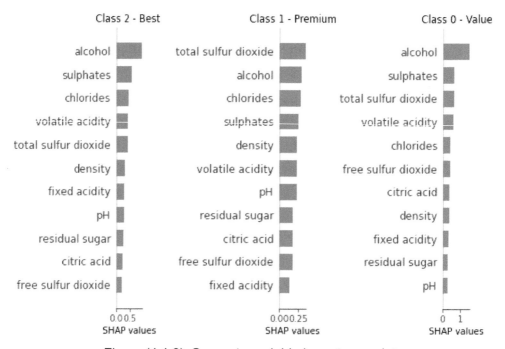

Figure (4.1.2): Separate variable importance plots

Conclusion

In this chapter we have learned various ways of presenting model predictions. They are all good options for you to deliver a stylized presentation. This effort pays off when your audience understands your predictions better and is ready to adopt your model.

Chapter 3: How Is the Partial Dependence Plot Calculated?

"Not all those who wander are lost."
~ J.R.R. Tolkien

In a linear regression, the relationship between the target and a feature can be easily observed by the sign of the coefficient. How can we discover the relationships between the target and variables in a machine learning model? The solution is the **Partial Dependence Plot (PDP)**. It shows the marginal effect that one or two features have on the predicted outcome. It shows whether the relationship between the target and a feature is linear, monotonic or more complex. It is introduced by J. H. Friedman [1], and has been widely applied in machine learning modeling.

(A) The Partial Dependence Plot

This chapter explains how the partial dependence plot is calculated. The definition of the partial dependence function is:

$$\hat{f}_S(x_S) = \frac{1}{n}\sum_{i=1}^{n}\hat{f}\left(x_s, x_C^{(i)}\right)$$

The machine learning model is $f(Xs,Xc)$. The Xs are the features to be plotted against the target to show the relationships. The Xc are other features and n is the number of samples in the dataset.

Let me explain the PDP step by step and illustrate in Figure (1). Assume a machine learning training dataset has three features ($X1$, $X2$, $X3$) and its target variable Y. See Step 0 in Figure (1).

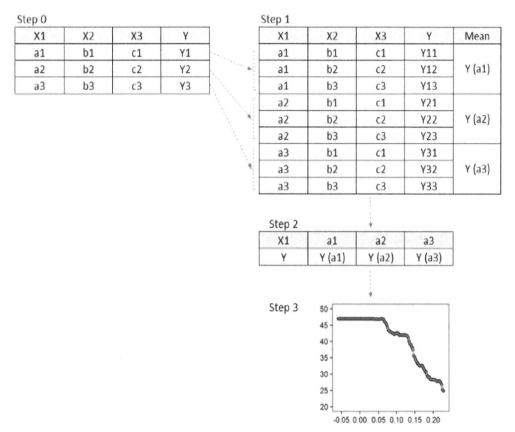

Figure (1): The step-by-step explanation

We are interested in the PDP to show the relationship between $X1$ and Y. We will first generate a new dataset as shown in Step 1. It permutes the $X1$ values with other real values of $X2$ and $X3$. Notice that the number of rows is expanded. (This step is done by the Monte Carlo method.) We then take the average of the predicted values (y_{11}, y_{12}, y_{13}) to get $Y(a_1)$. We continue to do the same for the value a_2 and a_3. This process calculates the marginal values for a range of X1 values (a_1 to a_3). The partial dependence function $fs(Xs)$ is shown in Step 2. Step 3 plots the PDP.

(B) Some Important Notes

Several important points in Step 1 are worth mentioning. First, the *Xs* and *Xc* are the actual feature values in the dataset. We do not impute any new values not in the training dataset.

Second, the permutation makes new records such as the second row in Step 1. The new records may not exist in the actual dataset. Why is this important? If there is strong correlation between *X1* and *X2*, a certain value *a1* may almost always correspond with *b1* and never correspond with *b2*. So, the averages in Step 2 may come from data points that are very unlikely to happen.

Third, which is the most important, if there is a **weak** correlation between the *Xc* features and the uninterested Xc features, the PDP will closely reflect the relationship between the target and *Xc*. This is mentioned in Friedman's paper: "The closer the dependence of *f(.)* on the subset *Xs* is to being additive or multiplicative, the more completely the partial dependence function *fs(.)* captures the nature of the influence of the variables in *Xs*." (for our readers, I use the notations in this article but not the original notations in the original article).

Conclusion

I dedicate this chapter just to explain the partial dependence plot. I hope the visual aid will help you understand on this topic.

References

1. Friedman, J. H. (2000). Greedy Function Approximation: A Gradient Boosting Machine. Annals of Statistics, 29, 1189--1232.

Chapter 4: Explain Any Model s with the SHAP Values – Use the KernelExplainer

"If your only tool is a hammer then every problem looks like a nail." ~ Abraham Maslow, American psychologist

In Chapter 1 and 2 we built a random forest tree and a XGB model. You may ask if there is a universal SHAP Explainer for any ML algorithm — not just tree-based but also for any non-tree-based algorithms. That's exactly what the **KernelExplainer**, a model-agnostic method, is designed to do. In this chapter, let's learn how to use the KernelExplainer for models built in KNN, SVM, Random Forest, and GBM.

(A) What Does the KernelExplainer Do?

The KernelExplainer builds a weighted linear regression by using your data, your predictions, and whatever function that predicts the predicted values. It computes the variable importance values based on the Shapley values from game theory, and the coefficients from a local linear regression.

The drawback of the KernelExplainer is its long running time. If your model is a tree-based machine learning model, you should use the tree explainer `TreeExplainer()` that has been optimized to render fast results. If your model is a deep learning model, use the deep learning explainer `DeepExplainer()`.

I will use the KernelExplainer for the KNN, SVM, Random Forest, and GBM models. I will repeat the following four plots for all of the algorithms:

1. The summary plot: `summary_plot()`
2. The dependence plot: `dependence_plot()`
3. The individual force plot: `force_plot()` for a given observation
4. The collective force plot: `force_plot()`.

```python
import pandas as pd
import numpy as np
np.random.seed(0)
import matplotlib.pyplot as plt

# Load the data
df = pd.read_csv('/winequality-red.csv')
from sklearn.model_selection import train_test_split
from sklearn import preprocessing
from sklearn.ensemble import RandomForestRegressor

# The target variable is 'quality'.
Y = df['quality']
X =  df[['fixed acidity', 'volatile acidity',
        'citric acid', 'residual sugar',
        'chlorides', 'free sulfur dioxide',
        'total sulfur dioxide', 'density',
        'pH', 'sulphates', 'alcohol']]

# Split the data into train and test data:
```

```
X_train, X_test, Y_train, Y_test =
    train_test_split(X, Y, test_size = 0.2)
```

(B) Random Forest

Let's build a random forest model and show its variable importance.

```
rf = RandomForestRegressor(max_depth=6,
    random_state=0,
    n_estimators=10)
rf.fit(X_train, Y_train)
print(rf.feature_importances_)

importances = rf.feature_importances_
indices = np.argsort(importances)
features = X_train.columns

plt.title('Feature Importances')
plt.barh(range(len(indices)),
        importances[indices],
        color='b',
        align='center')
plt.yticks(range(len(indices)),
        [features[i] for i in indices])
plt.xlabel('Relative Importance')
plt.show()
```

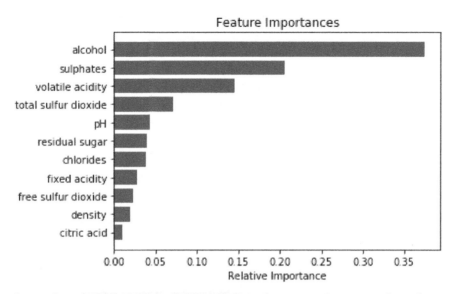

The function `KernelExplainer()` below performs a local regression by taking the prediction method `rf.predict()` and the data that you want to perform the SHAP values. Here I use the test dataset `X_test` which has 160 observations. This step can take a while.

```
import shap
rf_shap_values =
shap.KernelExplainer(rf.predict,X_test)
```

(B.1) The summary plot for the random forest model

Figure (B.1) is the summary plot by the KernelExplainer. You can compare it with Figure (D.1) in chapter 1, which is produced by the TreeExplainer.

```
shap.summary_plot(rf_shap_values, X_test)
```

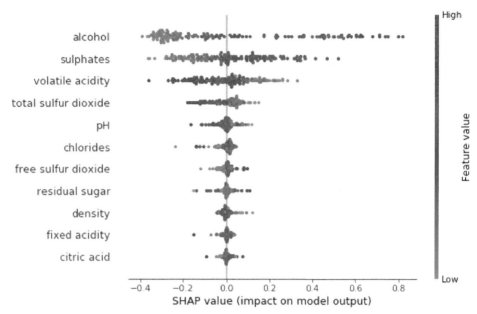

Figure (B.1): The summary plot for the random forest model

Let me just recap the description for the summary plot:

- *Feature importance:* Variables are ranked in descending order.
- *Impact:* The horizontal location shows whether the effect of that value is associated with a higher or lower prediction.
- *Original value:* Color shows whether that variable is high (in red) or low (in blue) for that observation.
- *Correlation:* A high level of the "alcohol" content has a high and positive impact on the quality rating. The "high" comes from the red color, and the "positive" impact is shown on the X-axis. Similarly, we will say "volatile acidity" is negatively correlated with the target variable.

You can save the summary plots by using `matplotlib`:

```
import matplotlib.pyplot as plt
f = plt.figure()
shap.summary_plot(rf_shap_values, X_test)
f.savefig("/summary_plot1.png",
          bbox_inches='tight',
          dpi=600)
```

(B.2). The dependence plot for the random forest model

A partial dependence plot shows the marginal effect that one or two variables have on the predicted outcome. We have explained how it is computed in Chapter 3 "How Is the Partial Dependent Plot Calculated?"

Assume we want to get the dependence plot of "alcohol". The SHAP module includes another variable that "alcohol" interacts most with. The following plot shows that there is an approximately linear and positive trend between "alcohol" and the target variable, and "alcohol" interacts with "residual sugar" frequently.

```
shap.dependence_plot("alcohol",
                     rf_shap_values,
                     X_test)
```

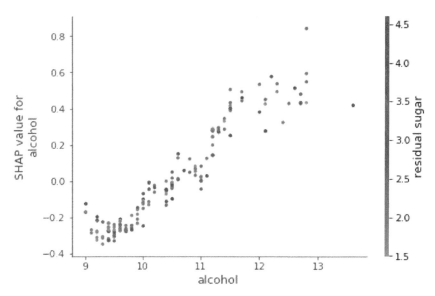

Figure (B.2): The partial dependence plot for the random forest model

(B.3) The force plot for the random forest model

A force plot shows which features had the most influence on the model prediction. The final prediction is the result of two competing forces. A red force means a variable has a positive impact and blue, negative.

I am going to produce the force plot for the 10th observation of the X_test. The values below are the averages of X_test, and the values of the 10th observation. Notice the "alcohol" level of this observation is 9.4, which is less than the average 10.48. We know alcohol positively contributes to wine quality. The fact that this observation has lower alcohol content tells us the wine quality will be lower and alcohol will become a negative force to the prediction.

74

```
X_test.mean()                           X_test.iloc[10,:]

fixed acidity          8.239375         fixed acidity          8.60000
volatile acidity       0.513281         volatile acidity       0.52000
citric acid            0.269812         citric acid            0.38000
residual sugar         2.557500         residual sugar         1.50000
chlorides              0.086425         chlorides              0.09600
free sulfur dioxide   14.981250         free sulfur dioxide    5.00000
total sulfur dioxide  42.506250         total sulfur dioxide  18.00000
density                0.996653         density                0.99666
pH                     3.318500         pH                     3.20000
sulphates              0.652063         sulphates              0.52000
alcohol               10.481250         alcohol                9.40000
dtype: float64                          Name: 1099, dtype: float64
```

```
# plot the SHAP values for the 10th observation
shap.force_plot(rf_explainer.expected_value,
rf_shap_values[10,:], X_test.iloc[10,:])
```

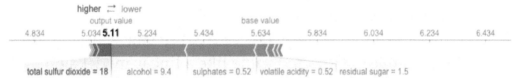

Figure (B.3): The force plot for the random forest model

Let's describe the story in Figure (B.3):

- ☒ The *output value* is the prediction for that observation (the prediction for this observation is 5.11).

- The *base value*: The base value E(y_hat) is "the value that would be predicted if we did not know any features for the current output." In other words, it is the mean prediction, or mean(yhat). You may wonder why it is 5.634. This is because the mean prediction of `Y_test` is 5.634. You can test it out by doing `Y_test.mean()`, which produces 5.634.
- ☒ *Red/blue*: Features that push the prediction higher (to the right) are shown in red, and those pushing the prediction lower are in blue.
- ☒ *Alcohol:* has a positive impact on the quality rating. The alcohol of this wine is 9.4 which is lower than the average value 10.48. So it pushes the prediction to the left.
- ☒ *Total sulfur dioxide:* is positively related to the quality rating. A higher-than-the-average sulfur dioxide (= 18 > 14.98) pushes the prediction to the right.
- The plot is centered on the x-axis at `explainer.expected_value`. All SHAP values are relative to the model's expected value like a linear model's effects are relative to the intercept.

(B.4) The collective force plot for the random forest model

Each observation has its own force plot. If all the force plots are combined, rotated 90 degrees, and stacked horizontally, we get the force plot of the entire data. In this section I will produce the collective forceplot for `X_test`.

```
shap.force_plot(rf_explainer.expected_value,
rf_shap_values, X_test)
```

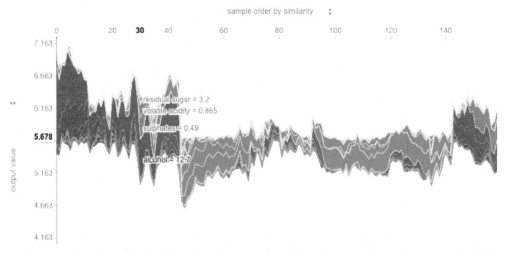

Figure (B.4): The collective force plot for the random forest model

The above Y-axis is the X-axis of the individual force plot. There are 160 data points in our X_test, so the X-axis has 160 observations. The average of all the predictions in `x_test` is 5.678.

(C) Gradient-Boosting Machine (GBM)

I built a GBM model with 500 trees (the default is 100) that should be fairly robust against over-fitting. I specify 20% of the training data for early stopping by using the hyper-parameter `validation_fraction=0.2`. This hyper-parameter, together with `n_iter_no_change=5` will help the model to stop earlier if the validation result is not improving after 5 times.

```
from sklearn import ensemble
n_estimators = 500
gbm = ensemble.GradientBoostingClassifier(
```

```
                 n_estimators=n_estimators,
                 validation_fraction=0.2,
                 n_iter_no_change=5,
                 tol=0.01,
                 random_state=0)
gbm = ensemble.GradientBoostingClassifier(
                 n_estimators=n_estimators,
                 random_state=0)
gbm.fit(X_train, Y_train)
```

Like the random forest section above, I use the function `KernelExplainer()` to generate the SHAP values. Then I will provide four plots.

```
import shap
gbm_shap_values =
shap.KernelExplainer(gbm.predict,X_test)
```

(C.1) The summary plot for the GBM model

When compared with the output of the random forest, GBM shows the same variable ranking for the first four variables but differs for the rest variables.

```
shap.summary_plot(gbm_shap_values, X_test)
```

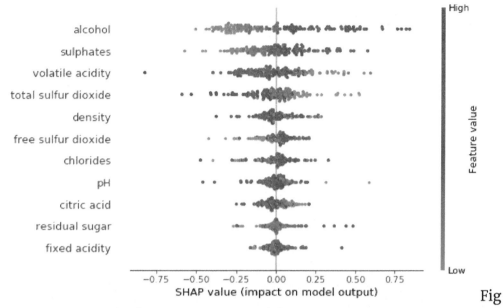

ure (C.1): The summary plot for the GBM model

(C.2) The dependence plot for the GBM model

The dependence plot of GBM shows that there is an approximately linear and positive trend between "alcohol" and the target variable. In contrast to the output of the random forest, GBM shows that "alcohol" interacts with the "density" frequently.

```
shap.dependence_plot("alcohol", gbm_shap_values,
X_test)
```

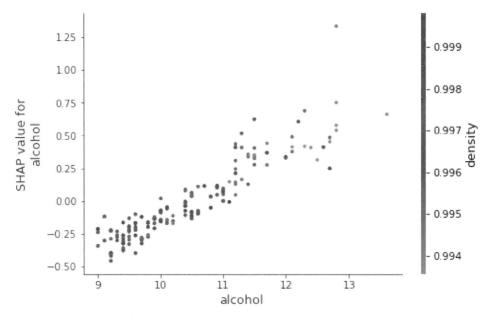

Figure (C.2): The partial dependence plot for the GBM model

(C.3) The force plot for the GBM model

I continue to produce the force plot for the 10th observation of the X_test data.

```
# plot the SHAP values for the 10th observation
shap.force_plot(gbm_explainer.expected_value,gbm_sha
p_values[10,:], X_test.iloc[10,:])
```

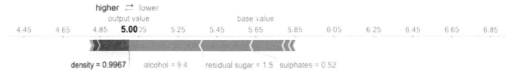

Figure (C.3): The force plot for the GBM model

The prediction of GBM for this observation is 5.00, different from 5.11 by the random forest. The forces that drive the prediction are similar to those of the random forest: alcohol, sulphates and residual sugar. But the force to drive the prediction up is different.

(C.4) The collective force plot for the GBM model

```
shap.force_plot(gbm_explainer.expected_value,
gbm_shap_values, X_test)
```

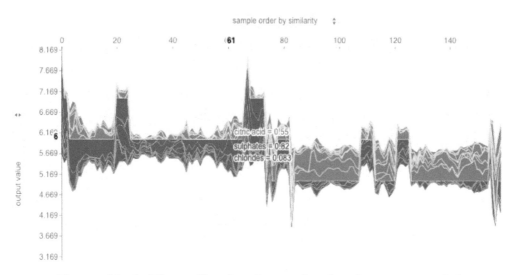

Figure (C.4): The collective force plot for the GBM model

(D) K-Nearest Neighbors (KNN)

Because the goal here is to demonstrate the SHAP values, I just set the KNN 15 neighbors and care less about optimizing the KNN model.

```
# Train the KNN model
from sklearn import neighbors
n_neighbors = 15
knn =
neighbors.KNeighborsClassifier(n_neighbors,weights='
distance')
knn.fit(X_train,Y_train)
# Produce the SHAP values
knn_explainer =
shap.KernelExplainer(knn.predict,X_test)
knn_shap_values = knn_explainer.shap_values(X_test)
```

(D.1) The summary plot for the KNN model

Interestingly the KNN shows a different variable ranking when compared with the output of the random forest or GBM. This departure is expected because KNN is prone to outliers and here we only train a KNN model. To mitigate the problem, you are advised to build several KNN models with different numbers of neighbors, then get the averages.

```
shap.summary_plot(knn_shap_values, X_test)
```

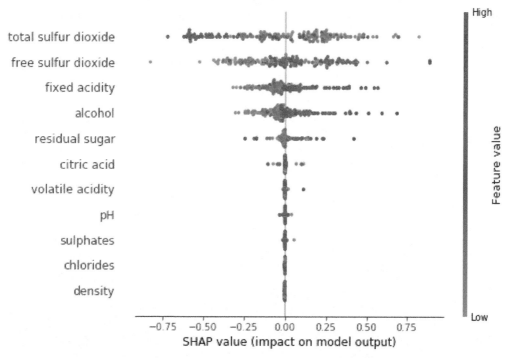

Figure (D.1): The summary plot for the KNN model

(D.2) The dependence plot for the KNN model

The output of the KNN shows that there is an approximately linear and positive trend between "alcohol" and the target variable. Different from the output of the random forest, the KNN shows that "alcohol" interacts with "total sulfur dioxide" frequently.

```
shap.dependence_plot("alcohol", knn_shap_values,
X_test)
```

83

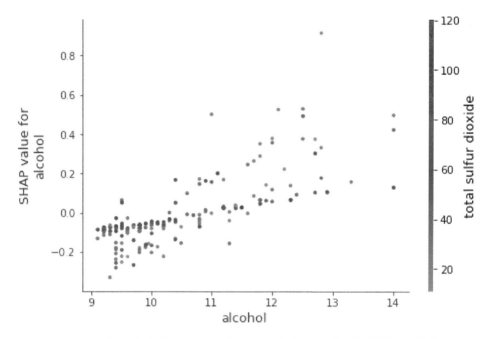

Figure (D.2): The dependence plot for the KNN model

(D.3) The force plot for the KNN model

```
# plot the SHAP values for the 10th observation
shap.force_plot(knn_explainer.expected_value,knn_sh
ap_values[10,:], X_test.iloc[10,:])
```

The prediction for this observation is 5.00 which is similar to that of GBM. The driving forces identified by the KNN are: "free sulfur dioxide", "alcohol" and "residual sugar".

(D.4) The collective force plot for the KNN model

```
shap.force_plot(knn_explainer.expected_value,
knn_shap_values, X_test)
```

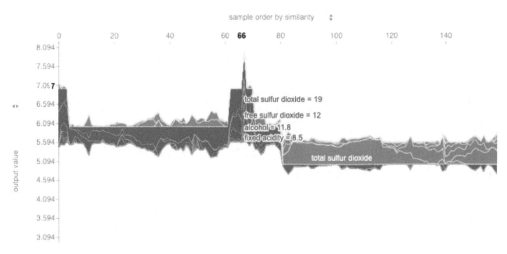

Figure (D.4): The collective force plot for the KNN model

(E) Support Vector Machine (SVM)

A SVM finds the optimal hyperplane to separate observations into classes. The SVM uses kernel functions to transform into a higher-dimensional space for the separation. (Note that the "kernel" functions in SVM have nothing to do with the KernelExplainer in SHAP.) Why does the separation become easier in a higher-dimensional space? This has to go back to the

Vapnik–Chervonenkis (VC) theory. It says mapping into a higher dimensional space often provides greater classification power. The common kernel functions are Radial Basis Function (RBF), Gaussian, Polynomial, and Sigmoid.

In this SVM model, I use the Radial Basis Function (RBF) with the parameter gamma. When the value of gamma is very small, the model is too constrained and cannot capture the complexity or "shape" of the data. Two options are available: `gamma='auto'` or `gamma='scale'` (see the scikit–learn api). Another important hyper-parameter is `decision_function_shape`. The hyper-parameter `decision_function_shape` tells SVM how close a data point is to the hyperplane. A data point close to the boundary means a low–confidence decision. There are two options: one–vs–rest (`'ovr'`) or one–vs–one (`'ovo'`). You can reference the documentation in scikit–learn.

```
# Build the SVM model
from sklearn import svm
svm = svm.SVC(gamma='scale',
      decision_function_shape='ovo')
svm.fit(X_train, Y_train)

# The SHAP values
svm_explainer =
shap.KernelExplainer(svm.predict, X_test)

svm_shap_values = svm_explainer.shap_values(X_test)
```

(E.1) The summary plot for the SVM model

Here again, we see a different summary plot from the output of the random forest and GBM. This is expected because we only train one SVM model and SVM is also prone to outliers.

```
shap.summary_plot(svm_shap_values, X_test)
```

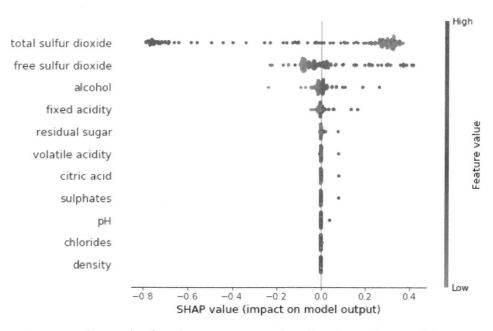

Figure (E.1): The summary plot for the SVM model

(E.2) The dependence plot for the SVM model

The output of the SVM shows a mild linear and positive trend between "alcohol" and the target variable. In contrast to the output of the random forest, the SVM shows that "alcohol" interacts with "fixed acidity" frequently.

```
shap.dependence_plot("alcohol", svm_shap_values,
X_test)
```

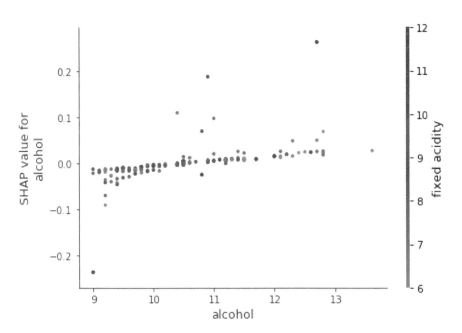

Figure (E.2): The dependence plot for the SVM model

(E.3) The force plot for the SVM model

```
# plot the SHAP values for the 10th observation
shap.force_plot(svm_explainer.expected_value,svm_sh
ap_values[10,:], X_test.iloc[10,:])
```

Figure (E.3): The force plot for the SVM model

The prediction of SVM for this observation is 6.00, different from 5.11 by the random forest. The forces that drive the prediction lower are similar to those of the random forest; in contrast, "total sulfur dioxide" is a strong force to drive the prediction up.

(E.4) The collective force plot for the SVM model

```
shap.force_plot(svm_explainer.expected_value,
svm_shap_values, X_test)
```

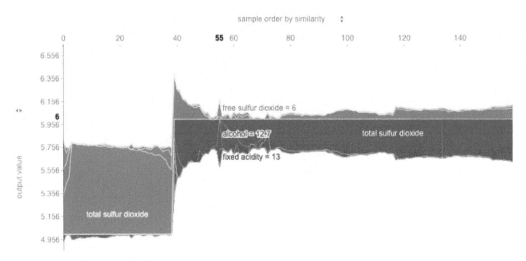

Figure (E.4): The collective plot for the SVM model

Conclusion

I hope this chapter gives you a good overview. In this chapter I showed you how to use the **KernelExplainer**, for different algorithms including KNN, SVM, Random Forest, and GBM. You may have noticed the variable importance ranking can vary slightly due to different modeling algorithms, thus the SHAP values can vary as well.

References

1. Friedman, J. H. (2000). Greedy Function Approximation: A Gradient Boosting Machine. Annals of Statistics, 29, 1189--1232.

Chapter 5: The SHAP Values with H2O Models

"There is a way to do it better - Find it." ~ Thomas Edison

The H2O Python module has been one of the favorite tools by many data science professionals. It is helpful to see how the H2O module incorporates the SHAP values. In this chapter I will explain what the H2O module is, how to use the H2O module to deliver model explainability.

H2O is an industrial-grade software for data modeling and general computing. This open-source, Java-based software features distributed (many machines), parallel (many CPUs), and in-memory processing. You can install the H2O open-source module with `pip install h2o`.

```
import h2o
h2o.init()

# Import wine quality dataset
f = "https://h2o-public-test-
data.s3.amazonaws.com/smalldata/wine/winequality-
redwhite-no-BOM.csv"
df = h2o.import_file("https://h2o-public-test-
data.s3.amazonaws.com/smalldata/wine/winequality-
redwhite-no-BOM.csv")
```

I will build a random forest regression model with H2O. I use the same <u>red wine quality data</u> as previous chapters. The target value of this dataset is the quality rating from low to high (0–10). The input variables are the content of each wine sample including fixed acidity, volatile acidity, citric acid, residual sugar, chlorides, free sulfur dioxide, total sulfur dioxide, density, pH, sulphates and alcohol. Notice the specific H2O syntax to do the train-test split.

```python
from h2o.estimators import H2ORandomForestEstimator

y = "quality"
x = ['fixed acidity', 'volatile acidity',
     'citric acid', 'residual sugar', 'chlorides',
     'free sulfur dioxide', 'total sulfur dioxide',
     'density', 'pH', 'sulphates', 'alcohol',]

# Split into train & test
splits = df.split_frame(ratios = [0.8], seed = 1)
train = splits[0]
test = splits[1]

# Build and train the model:
rf = H2ORandomForestEstimator(ntrees=100,
        max_depth=6,
        min_rows=10)
rf.train(x=x, y=y,
        training_frame=train,
        validation_frame=test)
```

(A) H2O's One-Line Code Makes It Easy

H2O builds the entire process in a pipeline. With only one line of code, you are going to see five exhibits:

- ☒ (A.1) the overall model variable importance,
- ☒ (A.2) the SHAP summary plot,
- ☒ (A.3) the partial dependence plot,
- ☒ (A.4) the individual conditional expectation plot, and
- ☒ (A.5) the residual plot.

```
model_explain = rf.explain(test)
```

(A.1) The Overall Model Variable Importance

The variable importance plot shows the relative importance of the most important variables in the model. Because we have interpreted the variable importance plot and the summary plot in Chapter 1,2, and 4, here I will just show the outcome.

Variable Importance

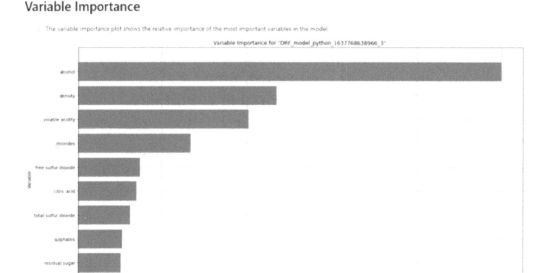

Figure (A.1) The Overall Model Variable Importance

(A.2) The SHAP Summary Plot

The SHAP summary plot show the positive and negative relationships of the predictors with the target variable. The description above the graph says:

"SHAP summary plot shows the contribution of the features for each instance (row of data). The sum of the feature contributions and the bias term is equal to the raw prediction of the model, i.e., prediction before applying inverse link function.

SHAP Summary

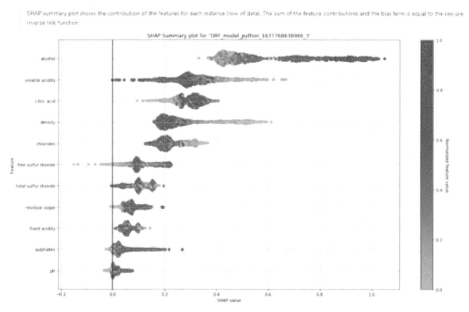

Figure (A.2) The SHAP Summary Plot

(A.3) The Partial Dependence Plot

Figure (A.3.1) is the partial dependence plot (PDP) by H2O. It may look different from the PDP in Chapter 1, which I reprint in Figure (A.3.2) for comparison. Basically Figure (A.3.1) delivers the same information. The X-axis in Figure (A.3.1) is "alcohol" and the Y-axis is "Mean Response". The gray bars are the histogram of the variable "alcohol". The description above the graph says:

Partial Dependence Plots

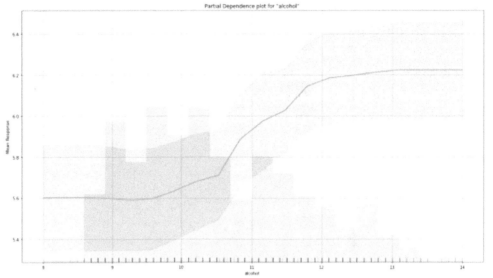

Figure (A.3.1): The PDP of "Alcohol" with the Target

"Partial dependence plot (PDP) gives a graphical depiction of the marginal effect of a variable on the response. The effect of a variable is measured in change in the mean response. PDP assumes independence between the feature for which is the PDP computed and the rest."

The green line, as well as its confidence interval, shows there is an approximately linear and positive trend between "alcohol" and the target variable "quality".

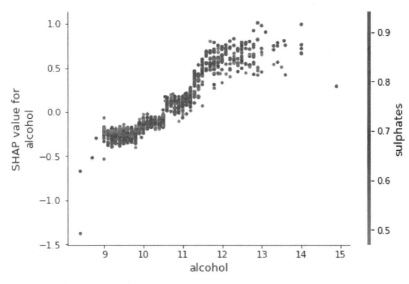

Figure (A.3.2): A reprint of Figure (D.1) in Chapter 1

Below The following plot shows there is an approximately linear and negative trend between "density" and the target variable.

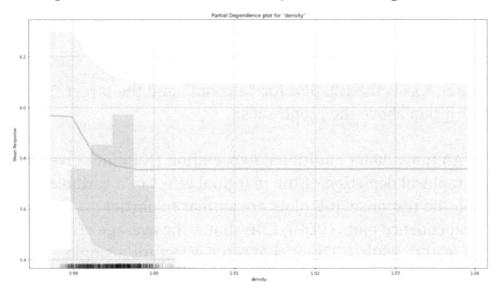

Figure (A.3.2): The PDP of "Density" with the Target

The partial dependence plot for the average effect of a feature is a global method. It does not focus on a specific data point (or record/instance). Section (A.4) introduces another method called the *individual conditional expectation.*

(A.4) The Individual Conditional Expectation Plot (ICE)

An equivalent plot to a PDP for individual data instances is called the **individual conditional expectation (ICE) plot** by Goldstein et al. [1]. An ICE plot visualizes the dependence of the prediction on a feature for *each* instance separately, resulting in one line per instance. If you take the average of the lines of an ICE plot, it becomes a PDP.

How are the values in an ICE plot generated? The idea is similar to the generation of a PDP. It keeps all other features the same, and creates small variants of the chosen instance. These new data points are fed to the model to produce their respective predictions.

Figure (A.4) is the ICE plot for "alcohol" and the target. The description above the graph says:

> "An Individual Conditional Expectation (ICE) plot gives a graphical depiction of the marginal effect of a variable on the response. ICE plots are similar to partial dependence plots (PDP); PDP shows the average effect of a feature while ICE plot shows the effect for a single instance. This function will plot the effect for each decile. In contrast to the PDP, ICE plots can provide

more insight, especially when there is stronger feature interaction."

First, we notice there are gray bars. They are the histogram of the variable "alcohol". Second, there are ten lines representing every 10th percentile. In the middle of the ten lines lie a dashed line (you may not be able to see it due to the small image). That dashed line, labeled "Partial Dependence Plot" in the graph, is the PDP line. These lines show the positive correlation between "alcohol" and "quality" – as the value of alcohol increases, the target value "quality" also increases.

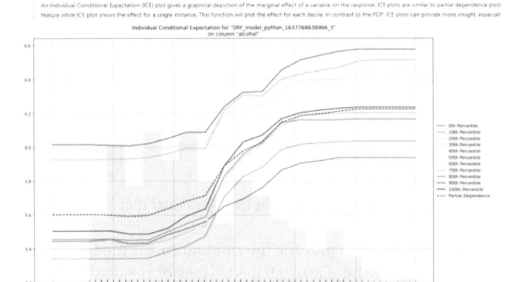

Figure (A.4): The ICE Plot

(A.5) The Residual Plot

Residuals are the differences between the actual values and the predicted values. If a model captures the patterns in the data well, there should not be any residual patterns left in the residual plot. Patterns can indicate potential problems that a model does not capture, such as heteroscedasticity, autocorrelation, and so on. We can plot the residuals against each input variable.

If we use a scatter plot to show the residuals on the Y-axis and the predicted values on the X-axis, we should see the residuals randomly dispersed around the horizontal axis. Figure (A.5) shows the ideal residual plot in the middle (marked by the green check). The other two graphs tell us there are still patterns uncaptured.

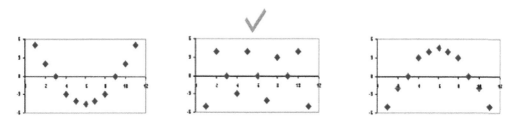

Figure (A.5.1): An Ideal Residual Plot

Below is the residual plot for the random forest model. You may feel strange why there are "striped" lines of residuals. This is because the target variable Y is an integer valued variable.

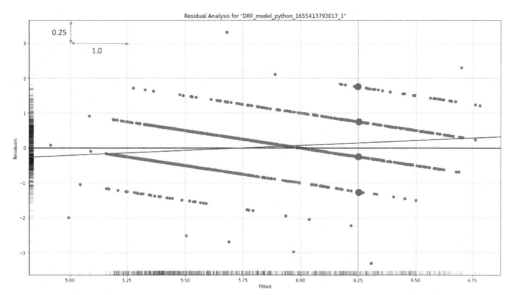

Figure (A.5.2): The Residual Plot

Let me explain further. Residuals are the difference between an observed Y and its predicted value. Because Y values are integers, the residuals for each integer value will line up along the integer values, and the residuals will have a slope of −1.0 on a residual plot. For any given X value (like 6.25), there are corresponding points (the red dots) on these lines. The average of those corresponding points tend to be zero. Notice the scale is 1.0 vs. 0.25 so visually the slope may not look like −1.0, but it is −1.0.

Figure (A.5.2) also shows residuals are parallel and roughly randomly distributed (along the integers). This is plausible. If these "error lines" are not parallel but dispersed with different slopes, the issue of heteroscedasticity may exist.

(B) Explaining More Observations with ICE

In the analysis below I identify the exact observation that was used in Chapter 1 (the 10th row in Figure (B)). Do you notice that I also include a few other records? While generating the small variants for the 10th row, ICE needs a few other rows to generate such small variants. If I do not include other rows, ICE cannot generate the small variants for the ICE plot.

```
obs = test[(test['sulphates']==0.64) &
    #(test['pH']==3.26)   &
    (test['alcohol']>10)
    ]
obs
```

fixed acidity	volatile acidity	citric acid	residual sugar	chlorides	free sulfur dioxide	total sulfur dioxide	density	pH	sulphates	alcohol	quality	type
7.5	0.27	0.31	17.7	0.051	33	173	0.999	3.09	0.64	10.2	5	white
6.6	0.16	0.32	1.4	0.035	49	186	0.9906	3.35	0.64	12.4	8	white
7.1	0.3	0.36	6.8	0.055	44.5	234	0.9972	3.49	0.64	10.2	6	white
7.1	0.21	0.28	2.7	0.034	23	111	0.99405	3.35	0.64	10.2	4	white
7.1	0.21	0.28	2.7	0.034	23	111	0.99405	3.35	0.64	10.2	4	white
6.7	0.34	0.3	8.5	0.059	24	152	0.99615	3.46	0.64	11	7	white
5.9	0.28	0.39	1.4	0.031	47	147	0.96836	3.08	0.64	12.9	7	white
6.5	0.16	0.34	1.4	0.029	29	133	0.99108	3.33	0.64	11.5	7	white
6.4	0.33	0.28	4	0.04	24	81	0.9903	3.26	0.64	12.6	7	white
4.8	0.13	0.32	1.2	0.042	40	98	0.9898	3.42	0.64	11.8	7	white

Figure (B): More Observations

```
rf.explain_row(obs, row_index=9)
```

(B.1) Explaining an Observation

The explanation for this observation is shown in Figure (B.1). The description above the graph says:

> "SHAP explanation shows contribution of features for a given instance. The sum of the feature contributions and the bias term is equal to the raw prediction of the model, i.e., prediction before applying inverse link function. H2O implements TreeSHAP which when the features are correlated, can increase contribution of a feature that had no influence on the prediction."

The prediction for this instance is 6.50. If you sum up all the SHAP values and the base value 5.81 (not shown), it will become 6.50.

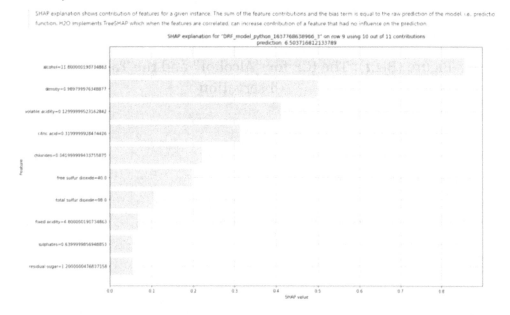

SHAP Explanation

Figure (B.1): The SHAP Explanation for the Observation

(B.2) ICE for the Observation

The interpretation for the ICE plots has been explained in (A.4). Below I only show two ICE plots.

Individual Conditional Expectation

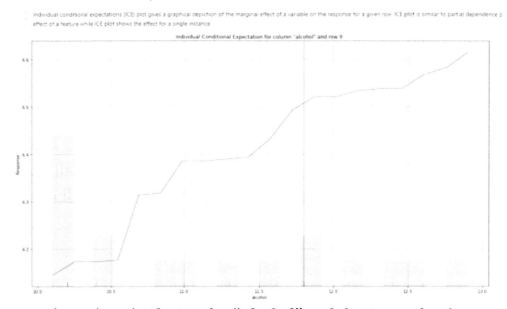

Figure (B.2.1): The ICE for "Alcohol" and the Target for the Observation

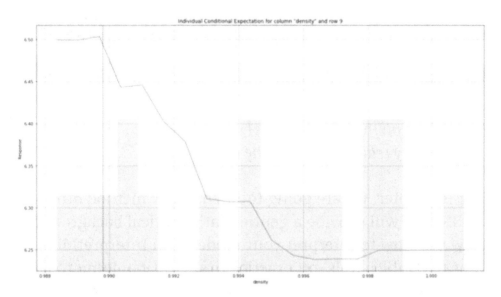

Figure (B.2.2): The ICE for "Density" and the Target for the Observation

Conclusion

I trust this chapter will motivate you to test the H2O module with SHAP. In the next two chapters, we will learn other methods to explain a model.

References

1. Goldstein, Alex & Kapelner, Adam & Bleich, Justin & Pitkin, Emil. (2013). Peeking Inside the Black Box: Visualizing Statistical Learning With Plots of Individual Conditional Expectation. Journal of Computational and Graphical Statistics. 24. 10.1080/10618600.2014.907095.

Chapter 6: Explain Your Model with Microsoft's InterpretML

"Beautiful [noun] [byoo-tee]
Is simply reality seen with the eyes of love"

In this chapter, we are going to learn a new method other than the SHAP. I will provide a gentle mathematical background then show you how to interpret your model with InterpretML. If you want to do the hands-on practice first, You can jump to the modeling part, then come back to review the mathematical background.

(A) The InterpretML Python Module

The InterpretML module was developed by a Microsoft team. The module leverages many libraries like Plotly, LIME, SHAP, SALib, so is compatible with other modules. Based on the Generalized Additive Model (GAM) and GA2M algorithms, the Microsoft team developed an interpretability algorithm called the *Explainable Boosting Machine (EBM)*. The development history from GAM to GA2M then EBM is quite inspiring. And I decided to describe it in this chapter.

(B) Understand Generalized Additive Models

The Generalized Additive Models (GAMs) were invented by Hastie and Tibshirani [1]. The GAM is an intuitive and powerful algorithm, though it does not receive sufficient popularity like random forest or gradient boosting in the data science community. Let me highlight the idea of GAM:

- ☒ *Relationships* between the individual predictors and the dependent variable follow smooth patterns that can be linear or nonlinear. Figure (B) illustrates the relationship between *x1* and *y* can be nonlinear.
- ☒ *Additive:* these smooth relationships can be estimated simultaneously then added up.

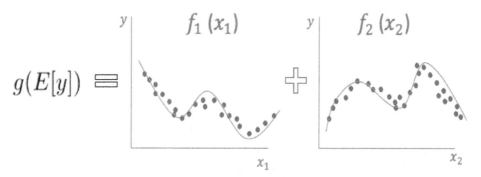

Figure (B): The Generalized Additive Model

In Figure (B) the *E(Y)* denotes the expected value. The *link function g()* links the expected value to the predictor variables. The function *f()* is called the *smooth* or *nonparametric* function. (*Nonparametric* means that the shape of predictor functions is solely determined by the data. In contrast, *parametric* means the shape of predictor functions are defined by a certain function and parameters.) When the function *f()* is linear, GAM reduces to GLM. GLM is easy to interpret, so is GAM.

If a GAM uses smooth functions to fit data, will it fit too well by specifying high-degree smooth functions? How do Tibshirani [1] overcome the overfitting challenge? They add an extra penalty in the loss function for each smooth term. They also apply regularization techniques such as LASSO, Ridge or Elastic Net. Therefore a GAM preserves the following advantages:

- It is easy to interpret.
- It is more flexible in fitting the data, and
- It regularizes the predictor functions to avoid overfitting.

(C) Add the Interaction Terms to GAM for Better Prediction Accuracy

However, the predictability of the standard GAMs is generally lower than that of more complex models. This is because the standard GAM does not have the interaction terms. To increase the predictability, Lou, Caruana, Gehrke, Hooker [2] add pairwise interaction terms to GAMs and call it *GA2M* — Generalized Additive Models plus Interactions. GA2M can increase prediction accuracy greatly, and still preserves its nice interpretability.

$$\text{GAM:} \quad g(E[y]) = \beta_0 + \sum f_j(x_j) \quad \text{Pairwise interaction terms}$$

$$\text{GA}^2\text{M:} \quad g(E[y]) = \beta_0 + \sum f_j(x_j) + \sum f_{i_j}(x_i, x_j)$$

Figure (C): The Generalized Additive Models Plus Interactions

(D) From GA2M to the Explainability Boosting Machine (EBM)

The pairwise interaction terms in GA2M increase accuracy. However, it comes with another problem – it is extremely time-consuming and CPU-hungry. The Microsoft team proposed a solution called *the Explainability Boosting Machine (EBM)*. The work is engineering. First, it trains each smooth function $f()$ using machine learning techniques such as bagging and gradient boosting (that's the name Boosting in EBM). Second, each feature is tested against all other features like a round-robin tournament. In a round-robin competition, each contestant meets every other contestant. In this way, the model finds the best feature function $f()$ for each feature and shows how each feature contributes to the model's prediction. Finally, EBM develops the GA2M algorithm in C++ and Python and takes advantage of joblib to provide multi-core and multi-machine parallelization.

(E) InterpretML — A One-Stop Shop

I call it a one-stop shop because it has incorporated the key modeling tasks in a pipeline. These tasks include data exploration, model training, model performance comparison, and prediction interpretability at both the global and local levels. In the following code example, I am going to perform the tasks in (E.1) to (E.6):

(E.1) **Explore** the Data
(E.2) **Train** the Explainable Boosting Machine (EBM)
(E.3) **Performance:** How Does the EBM Model Perform?
(E.4) **Global** Interpretability — What the Model Says for All Data

(E.5) **Local** Interpretability — What the Model Says for Individual Data

(E.6) **Dashboard:** Put All in a Dashboard — This is the Best

I continue to use the same red wine quality data. This allows us to compare the results of SHAP, LIME, and InterpretML. There are 1,599 wine samples. The column for the target is the quality rating from low to high (0–10). The input variables are the content of each wine sample including fixed acidity, volatile acidity, citric acid, residual sugar, chlorides, free sulfur dioxide, total sulfur dioxide, density, pH, sulphates, and alcohol.

```python
import pandas as pd
import numpy as np
np.random.seed(0)

# Load the data
# The target variable is 'quality'
df = pd.read_csv('/winequality-red.csv')

from sklearn.model_selection import train_test_split
Y = df['quality']
X =  df[['fixed acidity', 'volatile acidity',
        'citric acid', 'residual sugar',
        'chlorides', 'free sulfur dioxide',
        'total sulfur dioxide', 'density',
        'pH', 'sulphates', 'alcohol']]
X_featurenames = X.columns

# Split the data into train and test data:
X_train, X_test, Y_train, Y_test =
train_test_split(X, Y, test_size = 0.2)
```

(E.1) Explore the Data

Do `pip install -U interpret` to install the module. Then run the following code:

```
from interpret import show
from interpret.data import Marginal
marginal = Marginal().explain_data(X_train, Y_train,
name = 'Train Data')
show(marginal)
```

It presents a drop-down menu for the variables like Figure (E.1.1). When you click the "Summary", it presents the histogram of the target variable.

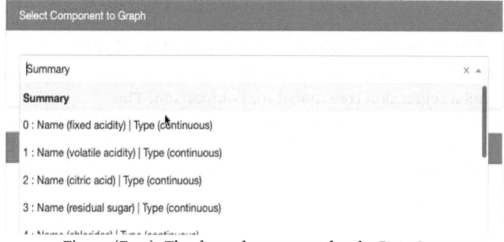

Figure (E.1.1): The drop-down menu for the Data Summary

Choose the first variable "Fixed Acidity" in the drop-down menu. The Pearson Correlation of "Fixed Acidity" with the target variable is presented. After the correlation value, the histogram of "Fixed Acidity" is shown in blue color, and the histogram of the target in red color. See Figure (E.1.2).

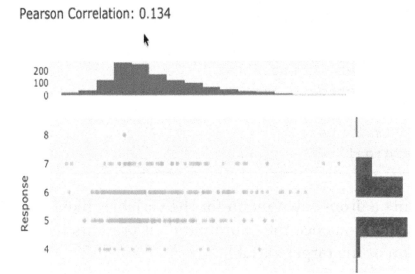

Figure (E.1.2): The Generalized Additive Model

(E.2) Train the Explainable Boosting Machine (EBM)

Besides building the EBM model, I also build a linear regression and a regression tree model for comparison. The `ExplainableBoostingREgressor()` uses all the default hyper-parameters as shown in the output. You can specify any of the hyper-parameters.

```
from interpret.glassbox import
ExplainableBoostingRegressor, LinearRegression,
RegressionTree

lr = LinearRegression(random_state=seed)
lr.fit(X_train, Y_train)
```

```
rt = RegressionTree(random_state=seed)
rt.fit(X_train, Y_train)

ebm =
ExplainableBoostingRegressor(random_state=seed)
ebm.fit(X_train, Y_train)
# For Classifier, use ebm =
ExplainableBoostingClassifier()
```

```
ExplainableBoostingRegressor(binning_strategy='uniform', data_n_episodes=2000,
                    early_stopping_run_length=50,
                    early_stopping_tolerance=1e-05,
                    feature_names=['fixed acidity', 'volatile acidity',
                                   'citric acid', 'residual sugar',
                                   'chlorides', 'free sulfur dioxide',
                                   'total sulfur dioxide', 'density',
                                   'pH', 'sulphates', 'alcohol'],
                    feature_step_n_inner_bags=0,
                    feature_types=['c...ntinuous',
                                   'continuous', 'continuous',
                                   'continuous', 'continuous',
                                   'continuous', 'continuous',
                                   'continuous', 'continuous',
                                   'continuous'],
                    holdout_size=0.15, holdout_split=0.15,
                    interactions=0, learning_rate=0.01,
                    main_attr='all', max_tree_splits=2,
                    min_cases_for_splits=2, n_estimators=16, n_jobs=-2,
                    random_state=1234, schema=None, scoring=None,
                    training_step_episodes=1)
```

(E.3) How Does the EBM Model Perform?

Use `RegressionPerf()` to assess the performance of each model on the test data. Figure (E.3.1) shows the R-squared value of EBM is 0.32. Figure (E.3.1) and Figure (E.3.2) show the R-squared of the linear regression model is 0.03, and that of the regression tree, 0.26. So EBM shows stronger performance.

```
from interpret import show
```

```
from interpret.perf import RegressionPerf

ebm_perf = RegressionPerf(ebm.predict).
        explain_perf(X_test, Y_test, name='EBM')
lr_perf = RegressionPerf(lr.predict).
        explain_perf(X_test, Y_test,
        name='Linear Regression')
rt_perf = RegressionPerf(rt.predict).
        explain_perf(X_test, Y_test,
        name='Regression Tree')
show(ebm_perf)
show(lr_perf)
show(rt_perf)
```

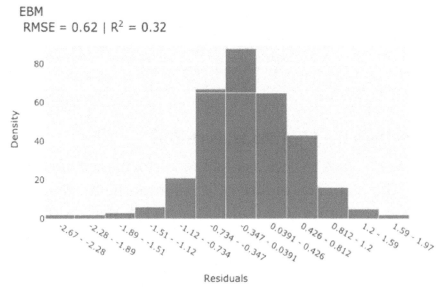

Figure (E.3.1): The EBM Model Output

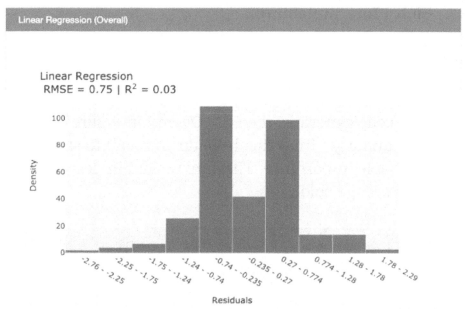

Figure (E.3.2): The Linear Regression Model Output

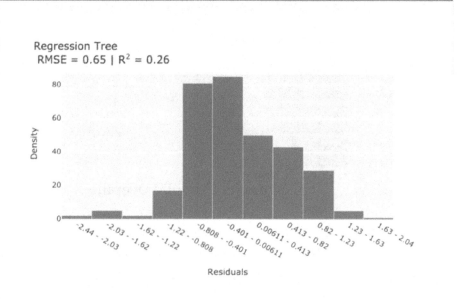

Figure (E.3.3): The Regression Tree Model Output

(E.4) Global Interpretability

```
ebm_global = ebm.explain_global(name='EBM')
show(ebm_global)
```

The above code generates the EBM Overall in Figure (E.4.1). Choose "Summary" from the drop-down menu to show the overall variable importance. They are ranked in descending order with orange color.

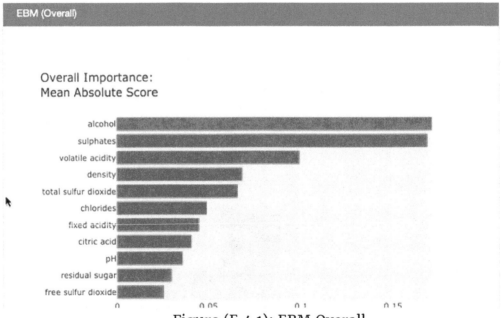

Figure (E.4.1): EBM Overall

Next, choose the first variable "Fixed Acidity" from the drop-down menu. Two plots will show up: the Partial Dependent Plot (PDP) and the histogram of "Fixed Acidity". The histogram indicates most of the values are between 6.0 to 10.0. The PDP shows there is a very mild linear and positive trend between

"Fixed Acidity" and the target variable when "Fixed Acidity" is between 6.0 to 10.0.

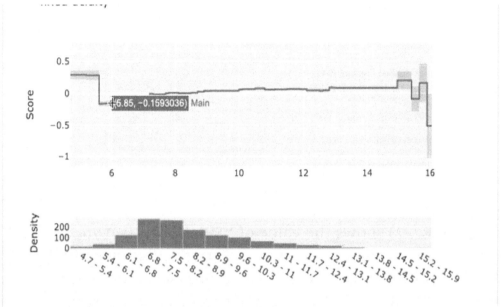

Figure (E.4.2): EBM Partial Dependence Plot

(E.5) Local Interpretability

Let's study the first five observations.

```
ebm_local = ebm.explain_local(X_test[:5], Y_test[:5],
name='EBM')
show(ebm_local)
```

The drop-down menu lists the predicted value and the actual value for each record. See Figure (E.5.1). Let's choose the first record.

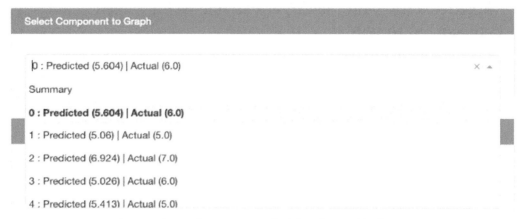

Figure (E.5.1): EBM Individual Predictions

Figure (E.5.2) shows the value of "Sulphates" is 0.76, and that of "Chlorides" is 0.17, and so on. The contributions of all variables for this record are ranked in descending order as below. "Sulphates" positively contributes to the target "quality", while "Chlorides", "Density", etc. negatively contributes to the target. Because EBM is an additive model like GAM, the prediction is the sum of all the coefficients.

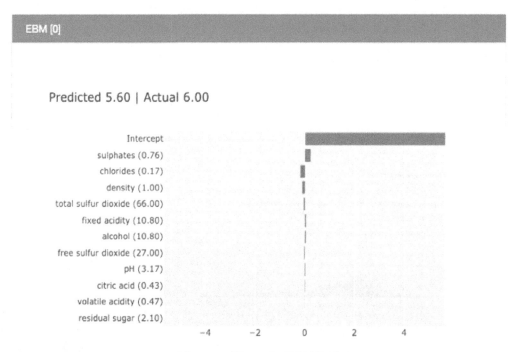

Figure (E.5.2): EBM[0]

(E.6) Put All in a Dashboard

All of the above can be put together in an elegant dashboard. Simply use a list to contain all the elements in the show() function:

```
show([marginal, lr_global, lr_perf, rt_global,
rt_perf, ebm_perf, ebm_global, ebm_local])
```

The dashboard's title is "Interpret ML Dashboard". It has five tabs. The first tab "Overview" is an introductory page. The second tab "Data" presents the same plots as described above in the "(E.1) Explore the Data" section.

(E.6.1) The Data Tab

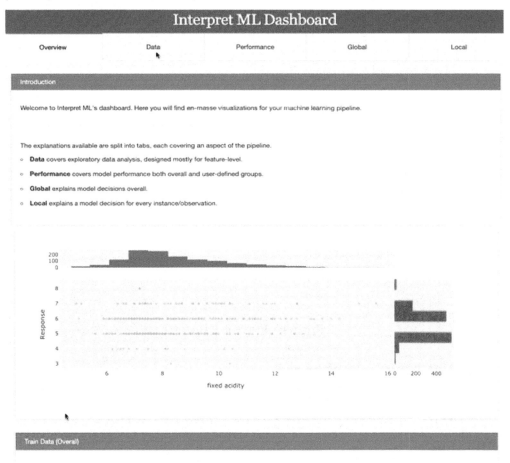

(E.6.2) The Performance Tab

The third tab "Performance" presents the same plots as described above in the "(C) How Does the EBM Model Perform" section.

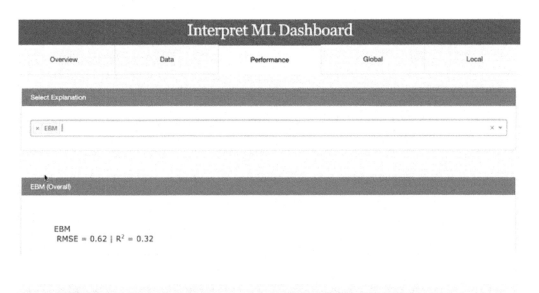

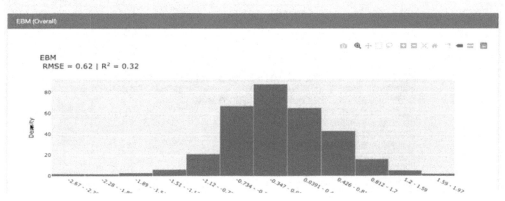

(E.6.3) The Global Tab

The fourth tab "Global" presents the same plots as described above in the "(D) Global Interpretability" section.

Overview	Data	Performance	Global	Local

Select Explanation

× EBM

Select Components to Graph

	Name	Type	# Unique	% Non-zero
	filter data...			
	fixed acidity	continuous	93	1
	volatile acidity	continuous	139	1
	citric acid	continuous	78	0.922
	residual sugar	continuous	84	1

EBM (Overall)

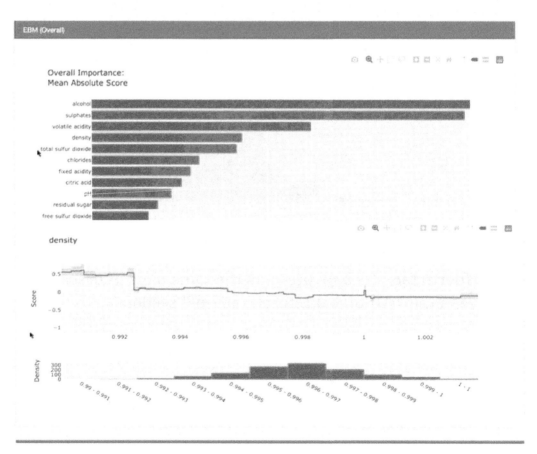

Overall Importance:
Mean Absolute Score

density

(E.6.4) The Local Tab

The fifth tab "Local" presents the same plots as described above in the "(E) Local Interpretability" section.

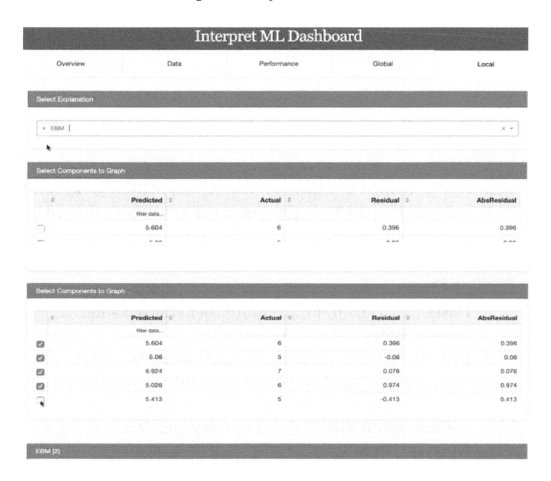

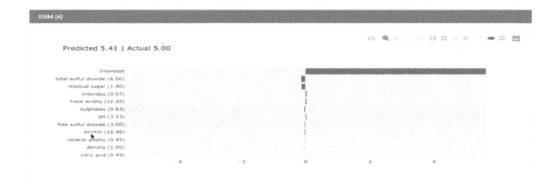

Conclusion

This chapter walked you through the development history from GAM to GA2M then EBM. It presented code examples that you can apply to your model.

References

1. Hastie, T., Tibshirani, R. (1990). Generalized additive models. Wiley Online Library.
2. Lou, Y., Caruana, R., Gehrke, J. & Hooker, G. (2013). Accurate intelligible models with pairwise interactions. Proceedings of the 19th ACM SIGKDD international conference on Knowledge discovery and data mining – KDD '13, : ACM Press.

Chapter 7: Explain Your Model with LIME

"When life gives you limes, squeeze and slice and add Tequila."

In this chapter I will introduce the LIME approach. I will start with the questions that the inventors of LIME were concerned with, then walk you through their solutions. You will see their arguments and motivations.

People typically agree that a linear model is more interpretable than a complicated machine learning model. Is it true? Do you think the following linear model is easily interpretable? Probably not. It has too many variables.

$$Y = 1.50 + 3.3\,X_1 + 25.4\,X_2 + 312\,X_3 + 32\,X_4$$
$$+436\,X_5 + 9.33\,X_6 + 2.3\,X_7 + 4.9\,X_8 + 0.3\,X_9 + 40.2\,X_{10} + 4.33\,X_{11}$$
$$+6.1\,X_{12} + 873\,X_{13} + 1.3\,X_{14} + 4.5\,X_{15} + 73.2\,X_{16} + 0.53\,X_{17} + 0.61\,X_{18}$$
$$+9.2\,X_{19} + 453\,X_{20} + 8.32\,X_{21} + 25.4\,X_{22} + 7.31\,X_{23}$$
$$+30.32\,X_{24} + 23.6\,X_{25} + 5.32\,X_{26} + 3.0\,X_{27} + 90.1\,X_{28}$$
$$+4.2\,X_{29} + 893\,X_{20} + 53.0\,X_{31} + 13.3\,X_{32} + 2.5\,X_{33} + 7.6\,X_{34} + 6.35\,X_{35}$$
$$+5.13\,X_{36} + 0.32\,X_{37} + 49.1\,X_{38} + 3.2\,X_{39} + 1.8\,X_{40}$$

Figure (A): A linear model with a lot of variables

Besides the above concern, the second concern is that this model has many variables. For an individual prediction, *only a few variables* play significant roles in the prediction. The rest variables are almost irrelevant.

These two questions are what Marco Tulio Ribeiro, Sameer Singh, and Carlos Guestrin, the authors of the paper "Why Should I Trust You?" [1], concerned about. Let's see their augments.

(A) Why Should I Trust You?

In their paper, the authors argue that we should build two types of trust for a user to adopt a model:

- **Trusting a prediction:** a user will trust an individual prediction to act upon. No user wants to accept a model prediction on blind faith, especially if the consequences can be catastrophic.
- **Trusting a model:** the user gains enough trust that the model will behave in reasonable ways when deployed. Although in the modeling stage accuracy metrics (such as AUC — Area under the curve) are used on multiple validation datasets to mimic the real-world data, there often exist significant differences in the real-world data. Besides using the accuracy metrics, we need to test the individual prediction explanations.

(B) "Easily Interpretable" and "Local Fidelity"

The authors of LIME argue that a model should be *easily interpretable*. The linear equation in Figure (A) is probably not easily interpretable.

Second, for an individual prediction there may be *only a few variables* influencing its predicted value. The interpretation should make sense from an individual prediction's view. The authors of LIME call this **local fidelity**. Features that are globally important may not be important in the local context, and vice versa. Because of this, it could be the case that only a handful of variables directly relate to a local (individual) prediction, even if a model has hundreds of variables globally.

In summary, the authors of LIME have two criteria for model explainability:

- **Easy to interpret:** A linear model can have hundreds or thousands of variables. Is it more interpretable than a complex gradient boosting or deep learning model?
- **Local fidelity:** the explanation for individual predictions should at least be *locally faithful*, i.e. it must correspond to how the model behaves in the vicinity of the individual observation being predicted. The authors address that local fidelity does not imply global fidelity: features that are globally important may not be important in the local context, and vice versa. Because of this, it could be the case that only a handful of variables directly relate to a local (individual) prediction, even if a model has hundreds of variables globally.

That's why they named this technique **Local Interpretable Model–Agnostic Explanations (LIME)** — It should be locally interpretable and able to explain any models.

(C) How Is LIME Different from SHAP?

In Chapter 1 I have described how the SHAP (SHapley Additive exPlanations) is built on the Shapley value. The Shapley value is the average of the marginal contributions across all permutations. Because the Shapley values consider all possible permutations, the SHAP is a united approach that provides global and local consistency and interpretability. However, the disadvantage of the SHAP algorithm is long computational time — it has to compute all permutations in order to give the results. In contrast, LIME (Local Interpretable Model–agnostic Explanations) builds sparse linear models around an individual prediction in its local vicinity. In short, the LIME is a subset of the SHAP. This interesting finding is documented in Lundberg and Lee [2].

(D) The Advantage of LIME over SHAP — SPEED

You may ask: "If SHAP is already a united solution, why should we consider LIME?" *The advantage of LIME is speed.* LIME perturbs data around an individual prediction to build a model, while SHAP has to compute all permutations globally to get local accuracy.

(E) How Does LIME Work?

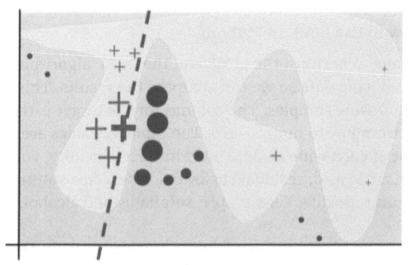

Figure (E): The LIME

Paper [1] has an intuitive graph as shown in Figure (E). The original complex model is represented by the blue/pink background. It is obviously not linear. The bold red cross is the individual prediction to be explained. The algorithm of LIME does the following steps:

- Generating new samples then gets their predictions using the original model, and
- Weighing these new samples by the proximity to the instance being explained (represented in Figure (E) by size).

Then it builds a linear regression for these newly created samples including the red cross. The dashed line is the learned explanation that is locally (but not globally) faithful.

(F) How to Use LIME in Python?

I continue to perform the LIME and the SHAP algorithms on the same red wine data so we can compare the results. This dataset has 1,599 wine samples. The column for the target is the quality rating from low to high (0–10). The input variables are the content of each wine sample including fixed acidity, volatile acidity, citric acid, residual sugar, chlorides, free sulfur dioxide, total sulfur dioxide, density, pH, sulphates and alcohol.

The purpose of LIME is to explain a machine learning model. So I will build a random forest model in Section (F.1), then apply LIME in Section (G).

(F.1) Build a model

```
import pandas as pd
import numpy as np
np.random.seed(0)
import matplotlib.pyplot as plt
# Load the data
# The target variable is 'quality'.
df = pd.read_csv('/winequality-red.csv')
from sklearn.model_selection import
train_test_split
from sklearn import preprocessing
from sklearn.ensemble import RandomForestRegressor
Y = df['quality']
X =  df[['fixed acidity', 'volatile acidity',
```

```
          'citric acid', 'residual sugar',
          'chlorides', 'free sulfur dioxide',
          'total sulfur dioxide', 'density',
          'pH', 'sulphates', 'alcohol']]
X_featurenames = X.columns

# Split the data into train and test data:
X_train, X_test, Y_train, Y_test =
train_test_split(X, Y, test_size = 0.2)

# Build the model with the random forest regression
algorithm:
model = RandomForestRegressor(max_depth=6,
        random_state=0,
        n_estimators=10)
model.fit(X_train, Y_train)
```

I am going to apply the model to the first two records of the test data `X_test`. The actual Y values of the two records are '6' and '5' from `Y_test[0:2]`. and the predictions are 5.58, 4.49 respectively by using `model.predict(X_test[0:2])`.

(F.2) Specify the LIME explainer

You will first install the LIME module (`pip install lime`). The code below builds the LIME model explainer.

```
import lime
import lime.lime_tabular

explainer = lime.lime_tabular.LimeTabularExplainer(
```

```
np.array(X_train),
    feature_names=X_featurenames,
      class_names=['quality'],
      verbose=True,
      mode='regression')
```

Why is it named `lime_tabular`? LIME names it for tabular (matrix) data, in contrast to `lime_text` for text data and `lime_image` for image data. In our example all predictors are numeric. LIME perturbs the data by sampling new data points from a standard normal distribution Normal(0,1) and scales the data according to the mean and standard deviation of the training data, to the appropriate scale. For categorical variables, LIME generates new data according to the distribution in the training data, then creates a binary feature of 1, if the value is the same as the instance being explained.

(G) Interpret Observation 1

Let's create the explanation graph for the first observation in `X_test`. The LIME explainer takes (i) the observation to be explained, and (ii) the model and the model prediction that needs to be interpreted. They are (i) `X_test.iloc[0]` and (ii) `model.predict` respectively. The LIME algorithm will generate new samples around `X_test.iloc[0]` and produce the predictions of those new samples using the model "model". These steps have been described in Section (E). The code uses `num_features` just to specify the number of features displayed.

```
exp = explainer.explain_instance(X_test.iloc[0],
    model.predict, num_features=10)
exp.as_pyplot_figure()
```

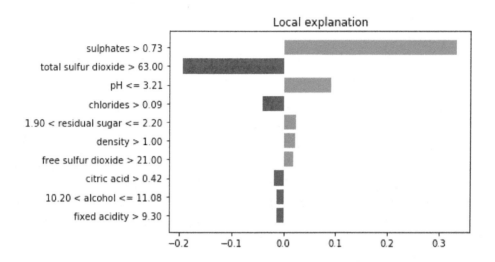

Figure (G.1): The LIME output for Observation 1 in X_test

Let's understand Figure (G.1):

- Green/Red color: features that have positive correlations with the target are shown in green, otherwise red.

- Sulphates>0.73: high sulphate values positively correlate with high wine quality.
- Total sulfur dioxide>63.0: high total sulfur dioxide values negatively correlate with high wine quality.
- ph≤3.21: low ph values positively correlate with high wine quality.
- Use the same logic to understand the rest of the features.

You can obtain the coefficients of the LIME model by `as_list()`, as shown in Figure (G.2):

```
pd.DataFrame(exp.as_list())
```

	0	1
0	sulphates > 0.73	0.333499
1	total sulfur dioxide > 63.00	-0.193760
2	pH <= 3.21	0.090470
3	chlorides > 0.09	-0.041554
4	1.90 < residual sugar <= 2.20	0.023432
5	density > 1.00	0.021439
6	free sulfur dioxide > 21.00	0.017841
7	citric acid > 0.42	-0.017636
8	10.20 < alcohol <= 11.08	-0.012900
9	fixed acidity > 9.30	-0.012791

Figure (G.2): The coefficients of the LIME model

And you can show all the results in a notebook-like format:

```
exp.show_in_notebook(show_table=True,
```

```
show_all=False)
```

Intercept 5.562429380784959
Prediction_local [5.7704678]
Right: 5.589345184970929

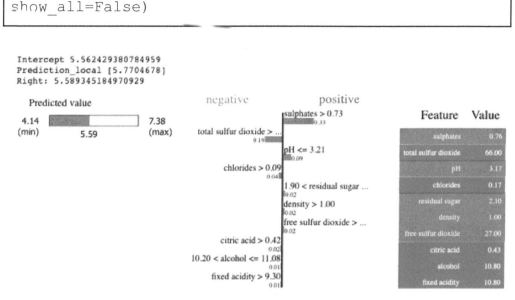

Figure (G.3): LIME outcome for Observation 1

- The LIME model intercept: 5.562,
- The LIME model prediction: "Prediction_local 5.770", and
- The original random forest model prediction: "Right: 5.589".

How does LIME get its Prediction_local 5.770? It is the intercept plus the sum of the coefficients. Because the intercept is 5.562 and the total of the coefficients is 0.208. It is obtained by `pd.DataFrame(exp.as_list())[1].sum()`. The LIME prediction is 5.678 + 0.208 = 5.770.

(H) Interpret Observation 2

Let me produce the explanation graph for the second observation in `X_test` just to see how it works.

```
exp = explainer.explain_instance(X_test.iloc[1],
model.predict)
exp.show_in_notebook(show_table=True, show_all=False)
```

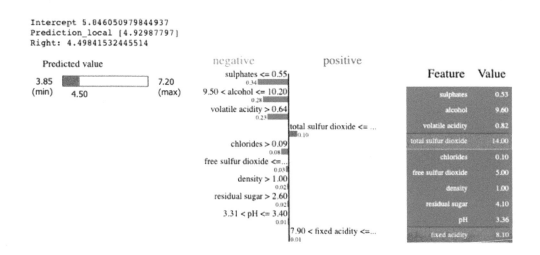

```
pd.DataFrame(exp.as_list())
```

		0	1
0	sulphates <= 0.55		-0.340787
1	9.50 < alcohol <= 10.20		-0.281007
2	volatile acidity > 0.64		-0.232907
3	total sulfur dioxide <= 22.00		0.095235
4	chlorides > 0.09		-0.082410
5	free sulfur dioxide <= 8.00		-0.032065
6	density > 1.00		-0.019631
7	residual sugar > 2.60		-0.018058
8	3.31 < pH <= 3.40		-0.014981
9	7.90 < fixed acidity <= 9.30		0.010440

The sum of the above coefficients is –0.916. Because the intercept is 5.846, the LIME prediction becomes 5.846 –0.916 = 4.929.

Conclusion

This chapter introduces the LIME method. It presented the questions that the inventors of LIME were concerned about. It walked you through the LIME method.

References

1. Ribeiro, M. T., Singh, S. & Guestrin, C. (2016). "Why Should I Trust You?": Explaining the Predictions of Any Classifier (cite arxiv:1602.04938)
2. Lundberg, S. M. & Lee, S.-I. (2017). A Unified Approach to Interpreting Model Predictions. In I. Guyon, U. V. Luxburg, S. Bengio, H. Wallach, R. Fergus, S. Vishwanathan & R. Garnett (ed.),Advances in Neural Information Processing Systems 30 (pp. 4765--4774) . Curran Associates, Inc. .

Made in the USA
Columbia, SC
21 December 2022

74803238R00076